Minnesota's Lost Towns
Northern Edition II

Also by Rhonda Fochs:

Minnesota's Lost Towns: Northern Edition

Minnesota's Lost Towns: Central Edition

Minnesota's Lost Towns: Southern Edition

Wisconsin's Lost Towns

Minnesota's Lost Towns

Northern Edition II

Rhonda Fochs

North Star Press of St. Cloud, In.
St. Cloud, Minnesota

ISBN 978-0-87839-805-8

Printed in the United States of America.

Published by:
North Star Press of St. Cloud, Inc.
St. Cloud, Minnesota
www.northstarpress.com

ACKNOWLEDGMENTS

Without the assistance, help, and support of many, many people and organizations, this book would not have been possible. Early historians, known and unknown, writing local and family histories left for later generations, an invaluable record of the times and people of the past. Their written works, letters, oral and written histories are a treasure-trove of memories, tales, anecdotes, and facts that would be lost without their foresight and their efforts to record them. Without their contributions, we would be severely limited in our knowledge of and the rich details of the past. It is a great debt that I—that we—owe to those early historians.

I can't stress enough the importance of local historical societies and museums. These local repositories are true gems right in the midst of our local communities. With limited funds and resources, the staff and volunteers of these organizations preserve our past and ensure our future. I urge you to visit them, support them and perhaps even volunteer. Without them, and the people involved with them, we would be sorely lacking in our historical knowledge and legacy. Libraries are equally important. This book could not have been written without them.

To my family and friends, I thank you for your belief, support and your help in so many ways. Special thanks to Marlys Vollegraaf, wordsmith extraordinaire.

To those that allowed me the use of their photos, thank you. Your credits are listed by your photos. A special thanks to T. Kremer. Your photos bring history to life.

Should I have inadvertently omitted anyone, my apologies. Any omission was purely unintentional. Again, thank you.

ORGANIZATIONS:
Beltrami County Historical Society
Carlton County Historical Society
Great River Regional Library
Helga Township
Isanti County Historical Society
Kanabec History Center
Koochiching County Historical Society
Marshall County Historical Society
MNLINK
Staples Library
Yellowmaps.com
http://alabamamaps.ua.edu/about.html

INDIVIDUALS:
Sue Adkins
David Aho
John and Lorraine Aiton
Laurel Beager
Gloria Beck
Dori Betts
Beryl Bissell
Judy Blais
Vanessa Bowen
Evonne Broten
Kent Broten
Jerry Carlson
Perry Exley
Renee Geving
Wally Glatz
Clifford Gustafson
Carol Harker
Fern Haugen
Connie Henderson
Thomas Holden
Sue Hosler Huber
Michael Kaiser
Judy Kangas
Dan Karolis

Tom Kremer
Marty Leistikow
Audrey LeVasseur
Larry Luukkonen
Rachael Martin
Cecelia Watters McKeig
Heather Monthei
Jeri Nelson
Jackie Nurnberger
Edgar Oerichbauer
Julie Riley
Cathy Salathe
John Schmidtbauer
Gene Schram
La Vonne Selleck
Brain Shultz
Ander Sundvick
Dan Turner
Leo Trunt
Sharon Vogt
Duane Welle
Clystrene Wilson
Marlys Wisch
Gerald Wollum
Betty Zaffke

Table of Contents

MINNESOTA GHOST TOWNS

Minnesota ghost towns are different. They are not the stuff of Hollywood movie sets nor the iconic "Wild West" images branded into our minds. They don't have the dusty tumble-weed strewn dirt streets lined with weather-beaten buildings. In the Midwest, our ghost towns are more the vanished villages, lost locations, abandoned communities and re-located town sites variety. I call them "places of the past."

In Minnesota, with our abundant natural resources, there are a multitude of these places of the past. Generally based on a one-industry, one-resource economy and the service-oriented support businesses, such as banks, retail stores, saloons, and brothels, the communities thrived as long as the industry or resource did. Once depleted, the industry owners moved to the next location, the supporting businesses failed, the residents moved on and the village faded, leaving few traces of its existence other than perhaps a wide spot along the highway, a clearing in the landscape, a crumbing foundation or two, decrepit weather-beaten buildings, and sometimes a cemetery. Disasters, wars, and changes in the area's economy also contributed to the loss of many towns and communities.

I've long had an interest and personal connection to the notion of ghost towns. My grandparents homesteaded in eastern Montana in a town that would fade into history in the 1920s. My aunt owned land upon which a booming early 1900s Wisconsin logging town was located. The town was abandoned after tornado and fire, leaving few remains.

In the 1970s my mother moved to Hackensack, Minnesota, and lived in a rustic basement cabin on Little Portage Lake. It was my first extended exposure to northern Minnesota, and it took root; I now live here full time and love it more each day.

To get to Mom's place I headed north out of Hackensack, turned west at the intersection of Highway 371 and Cass County #50. Every time we turned at the juncture, Mom would talk of a long-ago town that once sat there. While I had a fleeting fascination, I was young then and hadn't fully developed my love of history. I guess I didn't have enough of my own history to appreciate it as a whole. As years passed, I grew to treasure the past, eventually becoming a history teacher. But back then, I didn't listen as closely as I could have, should have. Not that Mom knew that much about the town, she just knew it used to be there and was intrigued by that fact.

Many years and lots of history have been added to my life since those days. Last year, as I marked a mile-stone birthday, the big sixty, I decided to indulge my interest, pursue my passion and make it my mission to learn all I could, locate, document and visit northern Minnesota's places of the past, those places where lives were lived, children were raised, homes and businesses were created and for various reasons were packed up and moved elsewhere.

This is the story of many of those towns.

WHAT IS A GHOST TOWN?

With no clear-cut definition, determining what constitutes a ghost town is highly subjective, often a matter of degree and opinion.

Purists will define a ghost town—a true ghost town—as a town that has been completely abandoned. Others argue that a ghost town is any community that is a semblance, shadow—or "ghost"—of what it used to be.

At its core, on a basic level, the most agreed upon definition would be that of a human settlement that has been abandoned. With an arbitrary definition in place it is possible to further classify ghost towns into categories or classes based on definitive characteristics.

The most common breakdowns and classes with Minnesota examples are: **

CLASS A – Barren site, nature has reclaimed the land, no visible signs of former inhabitation (Lothrop)

CLASS B – Rubble, foundations, roofless buildings (Gravelville)

CLASS C – Standing abandoned buildings, no/rural population, hamlet, no viable organized community (Gull River)

CLASS D – Semi/Near Ghost town. Many abandoned buildings, small resident population (Lincoln)

CLASS E – Busy historic community—smaller than in boom days (Rose City)

CLASS F – Restored town, historically preserved status (Old Crow Wing - Buena Vista)

A seventh category could also be included:

CLASS G – town joined or was absorbed by neighboring/thriving city (Spina)

Many communities, whatever their class, did leave behind tangible remains in the form of cemeteries. The hallowed grounds are a visible record of the times and lives of the town's inhabitants. Many areas also carry the town's name.

** Modified from Gary Speck's *Classes of Ghost Towns*

LIFE-CYCLE OF A GHOST TOWN

Minnesota, with its abundance of natural resources, has a multitude of used-to-be-towns—ghost towns. Generally based on a one-resource, one-industry economy, the population and all town activity would be heavily dependent on that one factor. The town survived as long as the resource did. Once it was depleted, the industry/owners moved workers and equipment to new locations and new opportunities.

The Michigan Chronoscope E-press describes the process simply and effectively. After the owners/industry moved on, soon the supporting businesses (retail, banks, saloons, brothels, hotels) failed, and the owners closed shop. Residents moved on to new lives, new jobs, homes, and communities. Some towns were dismantled, packed up and shipped out, reassembled in new locations. Others were abandoned and reclaimed by nature. Most left no physical remains except a cemetery or place name.

The earliest settlements first appeared along major transportation routes, primarily rivers. As time would progress, other transportation routes provided prime locations for a town, along tote roads or railroad lines. Others grew in haphazard patterns, when and where there was an opportunity. Native American villages were among the first communities. Though many were seasonal, there were some permanent villages. As settlers moved in, the communities became more permanent.

While each town or community was unique and had its own personality, there was a definite pattern to their life-cycles. The only variable being the rate of progression or pace at which a town moves(ed) through the cycle. Depending on the commodity or resource, this time frame could vary greatly.

Economists, sociologists and historians have labeled this a "boom-and-bust" economy. Models have been created that include definitive characteristics and stages of such an economy. Mining towns, particularly Western mining towns, were the examples most often used in setting the model. In large part, mining towns moved through the progression as a rapid pace. Moving at such an accelerated pace, it was possible to make observations that fit most of the towns that were products of a "boom and bust" economy. Michael Conlin, a business professor in Canada concisely lists the six stages of a "boom and bust" cycle in his book *Mining Heritage and Tourism*. The following are simplified modifications of his model as well as the process described by E-Press:

Stage One – Discovery and Growth
Resource is discovered and developed.
Size of the workforce is capped by workforce required to exploit the resource, often dictated by size and type of resource

Stage Two – Production
Highest level of activity

Stage Three – Decline
Production begins to decline—can be depletion of the resource or a decline in demand.
Can also be that costs have escalated making it unprofitable.
Decline may be rapid.

Stage Four – Abandonment
Owners move equipment and workers to new locations, closing down current production.
Supporting businesses fail/close shop.
Residents move on.

Stage Five – Decay
Town is either packed up or moved on, or buildings are left to decay.

Stage Six – Disappearance of Evidence of Occupation
Everything moved on or reclaimed by nature.

As the E-Press states, towns built on this model were doomed from the beginning to be ghost towns.

LIFE CYCLE BIBLIOGRAPHY

Conlin, Michael V., Lee Joliffe, ed. *Mining Heritage and Tourism: A Global Synthesis.*, UK, Routledge, 2010
"Ghost Towns of Newaygo." E-Press Chronograph Number II. Big Prairie Press. Winter 2007. Web. 16, Nov. 2012

GHOST TOWN CODE OF ETHICS

By their very nature, ghost towns are subject to the ravages of time and the elements. Harsh winter weather and humid summers in Minnesota all take their toll on the remnants of abandoned communities. Vandalism as well as accidental or unintentional damage adds to the deterioration of the sites. It is our duty and responsibility to treat these historic sites with respect and to do all we can to preserve the integrity of ghost towns. Use common sense and follow a code of ethics.

RESPECT PRIVATE PROPERTY.

Many former town sites are now located on private property. Please respect all private property.

Do not trespass—Do not enter private property without permission from the owner.

OBEY ALL POSTED SIGNS

Do not destroy, damage or deface any remains, buildings, or structures.

Do not remove anything from the sites.

Do not cause any disturbance to the foundations, vegetation, or land.

Do not litter. Remove and properly dispose of any trash you take into the area.

Always be courteous, respectful and SAFE.

TREAD LIGHTLY—TAKE ONLY PHOTOS—LEAVE ONLY FOOTPRINTS

Make as little impact on the environment as possible

Honor the past and preserve it for the future.

Aitkin County

Kimberly train depot. (Author's postcard collection)

GLORY

1901 - 1913

CLASS C

APPROXIMATE LOCATION:
Twelve miles SE of Aitkin on County Road #12

When the petition for a postal station was submitted for the community, several names were submitted. All of them were rejected. Trying one more time to find a name the postal service would accept, Glory, taken from the local men's quartet's favorite songs, "Glory Glory Hallelujah," was accepted by the postal service. The community became Glory.

Early settler Erick Swanson, as his daughter later shared, often made the eleven-mile trip to Aitkin. Neighbors often asked him to bring back small amounts of groceries and staple goods. After a bit, Swanson decided it would be easier to buy in bulk. Doing so he stored the excess groceries on a bench in his kitchen and soon his kitchen was overcrowded with shoppers. Swanson then built the Glory Store and soon he stocked a wide variety of goods. Vinegar and kerosene were sold by the quart or gallon out of a barrel. Pickled herring came out of a keg. The store operated until Swanson's death in 1948.

Today the area is still known as Glory. The Glory Baptist Church is active and strong. The corner is still referred to as "Hallelujah."

HAYPOINT

1900 – 1919(1980s)

CLASS C

APPROXIMATE LOCATION:
Minnesota Highway #169 and Aitkin County #7

The Haypoint area was always the center of activity from its earliest logging days. In the mid 1880s it was on the direct route for Native American wild ricing. The first white settler in the area, Joseph Tibbets, homesteaded at the site. He operated a store with a large dining room and kitchen. Upstairs he had a large bedroom with ten beds. Lured by advertisements touting farm-ready land, full of opportunities, other homesteaders began to arrive in the late 1800s.

A post office operated from 1900 until 1909. In 1900 a school was built across from the cemetery. A second school

Hayes Tavern, Haypoint. (Courtesy of Leo Trunt)

was built in 1906 and both schools later merged with Swatara schools. In 1910, Aitkin County drained its lowlands. In 1929, Highway 169 extended from Aitkin to Hill City, again putting Haypoint in a valuable, well-traveled location. The corners location was ideal for businesses. In the 1930s Hayes Tavern was there. The 1940s had an auto repair garage, hardware store and a cement block factory at the corners. The Willow Inn had gas, food and beer and it operated until 1974. In the 1970s the Haypoint Jackpine Swatara Snowmobile club was formed and tracks to Hill City were constructed. The region is still a popular recreational destination.

KIMBERLY

1879 - 1973

CLASS C

APPROXIMATE LOCATION:
12 miles from Aitkin on MN #47, left on 350th Avenue to 360th Avenue

Because of its location along the Northern Pacific Railroad line, Kimberly became the trading center and social hub of the region including the Thor and Fleming communities. It is said people came by horse, by walking and by skating and skiing to get their mail and supplies in Kimberly.

Settled in the 1870s, the community was named for Moses Kimberly, an early surveyor. The settlement was along the Rice River and the Northern Pacific Railroad line that ran from Duluth west to Staples. During its heyday, four trains a day, two eastbound and two westbound, plus a local route and the many ore trains from the mines ran through Kimberly. The Soo Line extended a line from Moose Lake to the mines in the area. That line was removed, and the Soo then hauled ore using the Northern Pacific tracks to McGregor, where the ore cars were then transferred back to Soo Line tracks.

A post office operated nearly one hundred years, from 1879 until 1973. An early news report (1922) wrote that the postmaster and the relief postmaster were killed in a hunting accident. The two men died from exposure after their boat capsized throwing them in the murky swampland. They were found the next morning waist-high in mud and muck.

Kimberly's heyday was in the early 1900s and the Great Depression years of the 1930s. With hard times, folks living in the city had difficulty making ends meet, so they headed to the country where it was possible to live off the land. Those years saw Kimberly's largest school enrollment, with two teachers required for the over fifty students. The school closed in 1962. The community also had three cream stations in 1930.

The area residents were hard-working and loved their dances. An Aitkin County history book tells that a concertina player from Duluth would come by train and play at all-night dances. A lookout walked the tracks and when the train approached, he raced to the dance hall, usually held at the Woodsmen Hall, to alert everyone that the train was coming. The dance abruptly ended as the musician raced to catch the train back to Duluth. The Woodsman Hall burned in the early 1920s. In the 1930s a store and feed room were converted to a dance hall. The crowds were so large that the feed room was torn down and an upright log hall was built. During World War II, the crowds declined, and the hall was torn down with the material used for a house on the lake.

Church services were first held in the homes of area residents or people would travel to nearby communities. A church was built in the 1920s but it was so hard to heat the building that no services were held from Christmas to Easter. That building was torn down in 1981 and a new church built in 1982.

The post office was discontinued in 1973. The area is still known as Kimberly and many people remember the community and preserve the history and the spirit.

LAWLER

1909 - 1964

CLASS D

APPROXIMATE LOCATION:
9 miles south of Tamarack Minnesota at intersection of Aitkin County Roads #13 and #16

The entire region was a tinderbox in October of 1918 and ready to erupt at any time. Not only had 1918 been an exceptionally dry year but the region had been in the grips of a severe drought for several years. It wouldn't, and didn't, take much for to set things off. As those familiar with logging life know, logging is not a clean, neat, compact business. Downed wood, scraps, dried timber, and brush are by-products of the timber industry and blanketed the countryside. Coupled with the fact that that, in the early railroad days, trains gave off

Troll Bar Stools, Jackson's Hole, Lawler. (Courtesy of Seth Hardmeyer, http://highwayhighlights.com)

Original Lawler telephone switchboard on display at Jackson's Hole. (Courtesy of C. Wilson)

Lawler Train Depot. (Courtesy of Dan West www.west2k.com)

sparks that often ignited fires, large and small, it was a tragedy waiting to happen. Add in the years of drought and dry conditions and you have a recipe for disaster. It all came together on October 12, 1918, near Lawler, Minnesota.

On that day, a spark from a passing train ignited the firestorm that is still considered the worst disaster in Minnesota history. The strong winds fanned the flames and the raging inferno burned east, sweeping the region on to Moose Lake and Cloquet, causing death and destruction in its path. More people (453) lost their lives on that one day than any

other day in Minnesota history. Over 52,000 people were injured or displaced. Thirty-eight communities were destroyed, including Lawler, which, except for the school house and Charlie Spicola's store, was decimated. One former resident, whose family has lived in the Lawler area for over one hundred years, tells that some residents took refuge in their fruit cellar only to fall victim to smoke inhalation. Those that sought safety in a nearby lake survived. Afterwards Lawler was apocalyptic. Everything was burned, trees smoldered for months and wolves howled and prowled, looking for food.

Lawler bank today. (Author's collection)

Lawler railroad building today. (Author's collection)

Lawler Hotel today. (Author's collection)

Before the fire, Lawler had been a booming town. Built on a logging/railroad economy the town included a railroad station, a school, bank, coop store, Charlie Spicola's store, a lumberyard, meat market, restaurant, stockyard, two halls (the Farmers Hall and the Temperance Hall), a store, which later became the Land O'Lakes creamery, a shoemaker/barber shop, a hotel, the Salo Telephone Company, and several other businesses that catered to the logging industry. A post office operated from 1906 until 1964. A school was built in 1916. It was a brick building and was quite modern. It had indoor flush toilets, a lunchroom, four large classrooms and a library. At one time there were over one hundred students.

Most of the early settlers were Finnish. Many had left their homeland because of hard times and the political oppression and unrest with neighboring Russia.

The Soo Line came through the area in the early 1900s and Lawler became an important trade center and hub. With a population of over 200, the town was thriving. Lawler was also

Lawler creamery ruins today. (Author's collection)

Spicola's store today. (Author's collection)

Gospel Tabernacle Church today. (Author's collection)

the social center of the region. Dances, plays and other community events were common and popular. One former resident recalls that the best years of her life were spent growing up in Lawler.

Some accounts indicate that the 1918 fire was the end of Lawler, but that was not so. Lawler was active and thriving in the 1940s and 1950s and in some ways, as far as community spirit goes, still is. With time, the bank became a tavern with pool tables. The Gospel Tabernacle Church was, as one former resident put it, a "Holy Roller" congregation. The co-op store is now Jackson's Hole, the present day gathering spot, watering hole and historical repository. The tavern has historical photos and artifacts including the switchboard from the Salo Telephone Company. One note of interest, Jackson's Hole also has very unique wooden bar stools. The stools are

Lawler marker. (Author's collection)

carved trolls and were created by a local resident, Cliff Letty, who was a woodwork artisan. Many original building still stand, and one is reminded of the iconic ghost town. It is important to remember, these historical buildings are private property, in tenuous condition and should not be disturbed.

The train tracks have been pulled up and the grade is now an ATV/Recreational use trail. An original cement structure stands alongside the former tracks. Historical markers detail the history of the community and the area. The new Salo Town Hall and Jackson's Hole are still active. Lawler may not be the trade center it once was, but it is still filled with a sense of community. Yearly events such as Lawler Days attract large crowds and includes dunk tanks, races, and more. Lawler as a town may be a "ghost" of what it was but not so the people and the legacy.

NICHOLS

1884 - 1926

CLASS C

APPROXIMATE LOCATION:
2 miles north of Garrison on U.S. #169, near intersection of 450th Avenue, shores of Mille Lacs Lake

When Austin Nichols was appointed postmaster of the settlement named for him in 1885, he was seventy years old and had lived quite an adventurous life. A former trapper and buffalo hunter from Iowa, he built a cabin and sawmill on the site of today's Austin, Minnesota. In fact, Austin is said to be named for Nichols. An Aitkin County history book states that Nichols may well be the only man in Minnesota to have two towns named after him, as well as other geographical features in the area.

After leaving Austin, Nichols's next job took him various villages and trading posts north and west of the Minneapolis/St. Paul area. One was near today's Garrison, Minnesota. Wanting the prime land for himself, Nichols applied for land patents in 1875, and in 1879 was awarded lands in the Mille Lacs Lake area. Setting up his homestead just north of Garrison and along the shores of Mille Lacs Lake, Nichols Farm or Nichols Place as it was called, soon became a popular destination.

Folks from Aitkin and from miles around came to Nichols Place and pitched their tents on Nichols shore line. They spent their time fishing and hunting. The land jutting out into the lake became known as Nichols Point and the surrounding water Nichols Bay. It is said that Austin also named several area lakes including Round, Partridge and Turtle.

With the establishment of a post office, Nichols also established a small store, a wood-frame school house and, for a time, a campground. Later cabins were added behind the store, where it was possible to rent boats, buy bait and get gas at the Pure Oil Station. The settlement also served as an area bus stop. Nichol's settlement with the cabins became the precursor to later resorts. Austin and his son, Frederick, are credited with establishing Aitkin County's first resort and the ensuing industry. In Austin's

old age—he lived to be 100—he moved to his son's homestead, just south of his own. Frederick managed the businesses. The store was later moved to Garrison. The school was burned by vandals, as was Austin's home, in 1990. The area is still a mecca for hunting and fishing and thousands travel by Nichols while in the scenic Mille Lacs Lake country.

RED TOP

1908 - 1954 (1960s)

CLASS C

APPROXIMATE LOCATION:
115th Lane off County Road #60

Red Top might well be the only lost town to have its own Facebook page. The page is managed, maintained and updated by part-time Red Top resident, Gerald Wollum. Gerald is the grandson of early settlers who arrived in the area in the early 1900s and in Red Top in 1913. He is also the author of a book on Red Top.

When the Soo Line Railroad came to the region in 1908, the town was surveyed with tamarack stakes. The corners of the town were marked with iron posts. Folklore tells that the

Downtown Red Top, 1919. (Courtesy of Gerald Wollum – www.facebook.com/redtopmn)

Early Red Top Post Office. (Courtesy of Gerald Wollum – www.facebook.com/redtopmn)

town was named for a young Swedish immigrant girl who worked as a cook in the area. She had bright red hair and was nicknamed "Red Top." The less interesting version of the town's naming has it named after the abundant red top field grass in the region. We may never know the true origin of the name as the original records have been lost.

Red Top was situated on a gravel plateau, said to be the only [usable] high ground between Wahkon and McGrath. A quarter section line road made the area accessible. The region's swampy landscape often made travel difficult. The Soo Line Railroad had crews working to fill in the low land throughout the summer of 1909. The crew took their meals in Red Top and it is said that Isle's (a nearby town) saloons were also kept busy.

Gerald Wollum writes that Red Top's boom years were from 1910 to 1920. The town's very first business was the Haggberg Store. The two-story building was constructed in 1908. In 1914, Haggberg's building became Hanson's Restaurant and Boarding House. Later a new store was built and the old building became a public hall among other uses. The new

store burned in 1924, and the old one reopened in 1926 becoming Red Top's last surviving business when it closed in 1951. The old store building was dismantled in 1968 and the associated house was burned in 1989.

In 1913, a new Soo Line depot was constructed in Red Top. Isle was a major railroad rival. Isle petitioned for a depot

Red Top Hotel, 1915. (Courtesy of Gerald Wollum – www. facebook. com/redtopmn)

Red Top depot with 2,000 rabbits. (Courtesy of Gerald Wollum – www. facebook. com/redtopmn)

Red Top Store, 1909. (Courtesy of Gerald Wollum – www. facebook. com/redtopmn)

Red Top Post Office. (Courtesy of Gerald Wollum – www. facebook. com/redtopmn)

Red Top Store, 1930s. (Courtesy of Gerald Wollum – www. facebook. com/redtopmn)

beginning in 1913 and finally got one in 1917. The Soo Line, seeing the possibility of more commerce in Isle, pressed the Railroad & Warehouse Commission to allow moving their agent from Red Top to Isle, which was approved. As Isle's rail traffic increased, Red Top's declined. A wide variety of items were shipped from the area including timber, potatoes, frozen snowshoe rabbits, cream, milk, and passengers.

Wollum tells that one rail agent also raised geese and bees. One day he went out to collect honey. He suited up with nets, masks, netting, and gloves. A short time later he returned howling in pain. Seems he had neglected to close off the rip in his trousers.

In later years, the depot was used for town dances and storage. It was torn down in 1940. A small depot was brought in and that stood until 1965 when it was moved to the Milaca area.

The community also had a Soo Line Stockyard, potato warehouse, church, and a blacksmith shop. The American Legion Post #354 was later rented to a barrel and whip factory. The Red Top Dance Hall was later at the site. The Hall had a kitchen and offered snacks. Local musicians and an old crank operated phonograph provided music. A wooden bench nailed to logs surrounded the dance floor. Many wild Saturday nights, fueled by locally available moonshine, were said to have occurred.

Red Top Store, 1930s. (Courtesy of Gerald Wollum – www. facebook. com/redtopmn)

Kalberg's Store was another local landmark. Wollum writes that the store had gas lights that burned all night. In 1924, those lights set the store on fire. Over one hundred residents fought the flames using water from the swamps, creek, and wells.

Hanson's Hotel, built in 1914 at Main and First, had a peaked roof, false front, and a stone-and-concrete foundation. As Red Top rail traffic slowed, the need for a hotel diminished as well. By 1925, the owners converted the hotel to a private home. In disrepair, the building was demolished in [circa] 1939, and the material was used to construct the White Cap Inn north of Isle.

Red Top did have a school but all school records were destroyed in the 1960s by the Isle School District to save storage space. The first classes were held in homes. In 1905 land was donated and a ten-by-twelve-foot log cabin was moved in and used as a school. In 1909 a one-room wood-frame school was constructed. It was later raised, and a basement was built. A pump organ and real slate blackboards were in the classroom. When the school consolidated with Isle in the mid-1940s the building was donated to the township and used for town business, meetings, and polling. Not wanting to be responsible for maintenance and upkeep, the town board declined repairs to the building. Deteriorating and vandalized for years, by 1960 the floors were buckling and the foundation cracked. It was torn down in 1968 for salvage lumber.

Many community groups were active and included the Red Top Farmers Club, the Red Top All-Star Baseball team, Ladies Aid, Young People's Society and many more. Unusual for the times, Red Top had a tennis court and a baseball field. In 1915 the court was graded using a steam tractor and the township road drag.

After forty-five years of operation, the post office closed in 1954. The end of the post office signaled the end of commerce in Red Top. As Gerald Wollum wrote, "Red Top may have faded as a town, but it is always a community."

ROSSBURG

1901 - 1937

CLASS A

APPROXIMATE LOCATION:
Five miles east of Aitkin on Aitkin County #5 near intersection of Aitkin County's #5 and #50

With a busy train station, stockyard, four stores, churches and a dance hall, Rossburg was, for a time, a busy trade center. Sunday afternoon baseball games were popular. With the dance hall and Woodman's Hall, Rossburg was the place to be on Saturday nights. Most of Rossburg's social activities centered around the community's two churches, a Catholic and a Protestant. Little remains of the community today.

SHOVEL LAKE

1910 - 1952

CLASS A

APPROXIMATE LOCATION:
Intersection of Aitkin County #67 (650th Street) and 426th Place, along Soo Line North ATV Trail

I first met John and Lorraine Aiton at my presentation in Blackduck. After the event, they came up to visit and to ask if I was interested in seeing the last photo taken of the Shovel Lake School. Was I ever! Showing me the black-and-white photo, they told me the story of John's father Harold, recycling the old historic school.

Last photo of Shovel Lake school, 1951-1952. (Courtesy of John and Lorraine Aiton)

Demolition of Shovel Lake school, 1951-1952. (Courtesy of John and Lorraine Aiton)

Harold lived through the Great Depression of the 1930s and also served in World War II's Battle of the Bulge. Both experiences most certainly shaped his philosophy and impacted his life and his perspective. Here in John's words (and John is a natural story teller) is the rest of the story, the story of his father and the Shovel Lake School.

Harold was at one time a county supervisor with the Farmers Home Administration in Grand Rapids. He grew up there and after college farmed in West Cohasset. John's mother was not fond of farm life and that, plus economic rigors of Depression-era farming resulted in renting out the farm and going with the FHA in the late 1930s.

Harold purchased the school about 1950. I don't know the particulars, but presume it was some sort of public sale. He gutted the interior, salvaging white oak trim, which he later sanded with a hand-held Sears belt sander. He used this for the interior trim. He also saved the joists and all other two-inch stock for the joists, rafters, and interior walls. He even saved the lath from plastered walls. He also saved the windows, and I imagine anything else of any conceivable values. "Wasteful" was not a term anyone used to describe Harold.

The school was built with clay tile/brick construction. Not long thereafter, buildings were built with frame construction surfaced with brick, as homes today. The structure started with clay tile, a bit like a narrower concrete block and the brick was laid with an air space between the two. I believe he had someone with a bulldozer knock these walls down before he knocked all the brick and tile apart with a hand-held masonry hammer. He purchased a used 1930s-era Chevrolet flatbed truck from the agricultural school in Grand Rapids to haul all this material to the building site. There, he cleaned the excess mortar from each brick and each tile, one by one, with the masonry hammer, a wire brush, and muriatic acid, pretty much by himself.

Shovel Lake School as a private home. (Courtesy of John and Lorraine Aiton)

The process took two years. The photo is dated 1951, but I believe it was taken a year earlier and not developed until the next year. It shows an intact superstructure, complete with windows. The new house, contractor built, was completed in 1952 and we moved in in September of that year. It was about 2,000 square feet with a single, attached garage, basement apartment, brick terrace patio, brick sidewalks, all from the school. Brick/tile construction was used, as in the school, with plaster and lath (from the school) interior walls causing the place to resemble a kiln in the summer as there wasn't a tree on the lot for shade and the roof was dark-brown absorbing the heat. It was a rather deluxe home for the time, and it still stands on Pokegama Avenue, South #169 two blocks south of the Mississippi River Bridge.

Unused materials and the truck were sold.

As John relates, this was a back-breaking task and maybe more. John's mother often said the Harold was "never the same." It was a major undertaking and illustrates the will of one man who in his way, recycled history.

SWATARA

1903 - 1984

CLASS D

APPROXIMATE LOCATION:
Junction of Aitkin County Roads #7 and #29

No one knows for sure why the community was named Swatara. The 1913 petition for postal service was submitted as "Boydsville" after James Boyd, an early settler. That name was rejected and the postal service assigned the name "Swatara" with no explanation or reasons. Some believed it might be a Native American word meaning "two rivers," which would be fitting as Swatara was by two rivers. But no credible sources could substantiate that explanation. Another possibility was that the name of the community was derived from Swatara Township in Pennsylvania. We most likely will never know.

Swatara began as a supply station for the region's lumber camps and as a siding for the Soo Line Railroad. When the

Soo Line came through in 1910, it constructed a station house, passenger platform, two-stall outhouse, a depot, stockyard, and feed racks. A full-time agent was hired in 1915.

In 1910, Boyd and Young brought carloads of groceries and hardware into the camps, but also sold to area residents. They later moved to Swatara and built a store. The store building was an all-purpose one and was also used as a community hall. The twenty-four-by-sixty-foot building housed the groceries and hardware on the ground floor and the hall on the second floor. Dances were held on Saturday nights and church services on Sundays.

A two-story school building was constructed in the 1920s and replaced the original tar paper shack of a school built in 1913. The new school was brick and concrete. The school had four teachers, four rooms, showers, and its own power plant run by a gasoline engine located in the basement. The first school buses were REO Speed Wagons with wooden Wayne

Swatara Main Post Office. (Author's collection)

Swatara Main Post Office flag. (Author's collection)

My Address is Still

Swatara

Have You Forgotten it

Swatara Main Street ca 1910. (Author's collection)

Swatara, 1986. (Author's collection, courtesy of R. Franklin)

bodies. They were used for eleven years. Due to declining enrollment the high school program was discontinued in 1925.

Boyd and Young's weren't the only stores in the community. Another was the Trepanier Store. Trepaniers also operated a hotel until the 1930s. The hotel had a pool hall in the basement. Heath Brothers was another store. The brothers were also undertakers so there were a number of caskets in the back of the store.

The Immaculate Conception Catholic Church was built in 1916 and in 1929 it was renamed St. James. It closed in 1993. A Methodist Church was also established in the community.

A bank operated in the Swatara community. It later merged with Shovel Lake and lastly with the bank in Remer, which is still in operation. Other community businesses were a lunch counter, confectionary store, barber shop, bakery, and pool hall. After the bank closed, the building was used as a tavern. A community newspaper, *The Swatara Sweepstakes* operated for nineteen issues, but there just weren't enough sales to keep it going.

The 1930s dealt Swatara a double blow. Highway #35 was rebuilt and relocated just to the east of Swatara, through Haypoint. The loss of traffic traveling through town was a significant blow. In addition, the Great Depression dealt the community a financial blow from which it just couldn't recover.

A crate factory was in operation in the 1940s. In 1958, the Soo Line petitioned to close all operations in Swatara. That petition was rejected. In 1959, passenger service was discontinued. In 1972 the depot was officially closed. The last train ran over the tracks in 1985. Then the tracks were torn up. The depot building burned in 1987. Today the right-of-way is owned by Aitkin County and the old grade is used as a snowmobile trail.

The school merged with Hill City in the early 1970s. The Swatara School was used as an elementary school for many years. When a new Hill City school was built in 1983, the Swatara School was closed. The post office was discontinued in 1984. Things had certainly quieted down in Swatara since its early days but in 1969, things got lively. Swatara was chosen as the site for the proposed Minnesota Experimental City or MXC. The whole concept seems like something out of science fiction.

Briefly, in 1969, the Minnesota Legislature authorized a study of the MXC as conceived by Dr. Atheistan Spilhaus. A joint committee was assigned and the project would consist of five phases.

The second phase was authorized by the Minnesota Legislature in 1971. An eleven-member MXC Authority was charged with planning the various needs of the city and selecting a site. They had $250,000,000.00 dollars to work with. The group, with the University of Minnesota and the business sector, included the Ford Motor Company, which donated $300,000 for the transportation study alone. Ford was looking for new kinds of cars, how to move them and a monorail system. Criteria were developed for the selection of sites for the proposed city. They decided on two locations.

One was near Evansville in Douglas County and was called the "Lake Region" site. "Pine Moraine" was the other site and it was near Swatara and included much of Northeastern Aitkin County and part of Northeastern Cass County. The Swatara site was their final choice.

The plan was to have an urban core surrounded by a less densely crowded area that would serve as the residential district. A green buffer would also be included. Advocates all over the country were in favor of the concept, at first.

The Aitkin County Board endorsed the plan by a 5 to 0 vote. They thought it would be good for the county and would create much needed jobs. In the Swatara area, the mood was mixed. At first many approved of the idea. As time went on, the number of those opposed grew. The main reason for opposition was that people didn't think it could be built without destroying the environment. An opposition group, "Save Our Northland" was formed. Hearings were held and all the while, tensions increased. It all came to a head in January 1973 when a group of opponents walked from Swatara to the Minnesota State Capitol in St. Paul. Legislative hearings were packed with opponents. The Minnesota Pollution Control Board voted 81 to 1 against appropriating the money for the land purchase. The project was dead.

Many wonder if the project was killed by the opposition or did it die due to the exorbitant costs estimated to be 10 to 15 billion dollars at a minimum. America's conservative and cutback landscape also helped nix the project. The Minnesota Legislature was more concerned with financing the Metrodome than it was in building an experimental city.

After the hoopla, Swatara continued on. Over the years the post office closed, the school closed, and most businesses closed. The railroad ceased operations, and the tracks were pulled up. Still Swatara is community-minded and treasures its natural beauty and its recreational opportunities.

THOR

1904 - 1937

CLASS A

APPROXIMATE LOCATION:
16 miles SE of Aitkin on County Road #4 (Dam Lake Street)

In Thor's early days, mail was delivered twice a week to the post office which operated from 1904 to 1937. A later postmaster put in a line of groceries for area residents convenience. The general store operated until 1975. The Thor Lutheran Church was active for many years.

Becker County

McHugh 2014. (Author's collection)

McHugh today. (Author's collection)

McHugh

1887 - 1918 (1970s)

CLASS A

APPROXIMATE LOCATION:
4 miles east of Detroit Lakes on north side of Highway 10 &
McHugh Road

Botany and bicycles are widely disparate disciplines yet the two share a common bond with the Village of McHugh, just four miles east of Detroit Lakes in Becker County. Reverend Chandonnetii of Perham was an early 1900s botanist and spent much of his free time gathering plant specimens for his collection. In June of 1911, he was scouting the McHugh area, around the railroad yard and came upon a previously undescribed and unnamed perennial of the milkvetch (pea) family. His collection notes state it was collected in "dry soil at railroad yard McHugh, near Detroit, MN." An *American Naturalist* article states that as was usual, the plant was later named after its discoverer and became known as Astragalus Chardonnetii.

As for bicycles, in the late 1890s, Lewis Harper operated a bicycle factory in McHugh. Further research reveals more about Harper and his bicycles. Innovative and creative, Harper is an important pioneer in bicycle history. Focusing more on monocycles than bicycles, Harper patented at least two of his designs. A July 18, 1893, patent for a velocipede saddle, Pat. #501,782, and in December of 1893, Pat. #511,139, for a unicycle. One online resource (www.monowheels.com) states that Harper demonstrated his monocycle in England at a velo expedition. Said to have achieved an "unheard of speed" of thirty miles per hour, Harper was awarded a prize. Returning

to America to promote his invention, he was severely injured at the first public appearance. There seems to be discussion as to the originality of monowheel designs. Nonetheless, Harper played an important role in early bicycle history.

The old village of McHugh was first settled in the 1870s. A Northern Pacific rail station was established in 1887. The railroad station was in direct response to the area's abundant wood resources. Fence posts and railroad ties were major industries in McHugh. Brick making was also an important industry. The McHugh Brick Company was established by William Sherman and it produced hundreds of thousands of bricks each year during its fifteen-year existence (1900 to 1915). Sherman also operated the McHugh Hotel. Though small it was busy with railroad travelers and because of its location on the busy road—later U.S. Highway 10. The hotel building was later used as a private residence.

A post office began in 1887 and operated until 1918. The town also had a store and a school. The community lasted

Harpers Monowheel. (Courtesy of www.monowheels,com)

Original McHugh sign at the Becker County Historical Society. (Author's collection)

until the later twentieth century. Area residents Willma Hanson and Gary Nelson have conducted detailed research on the town. Gary was born in McHugh and lived there until the late 1970s and Willma still lives in the area.

As rail traffic declined and auto use became the primary transportation method, Highway 10 continued to be enlarged and expanded into the major thoroughfare it is today. The old road, just to the north of Highway 10 (at McHugh Road) routes through the old town site. The rail tracks are still there, and it is possible to walk the crumling blacktop and the old streets of long ago McHugh.

MIDWAY

1913 – 1938 (1960s)

CLASS A

APPROXIMATE LOCATION:
28 Miles East of Detroit Lakes on Highway 47

With a name like "Midway," one would guess that the town was centrally located halfway between two points. That it was! Located midway between Wolf Lake and Menagha, the community had a creamery, grocery store, and a post office from 1913 to 1931. The first store was built in 1914 and it was destroyed by fire in 1926. It was rebuilt that same year. Electricity came to the region in 1944. The community was known for its baseball team which began in the 1950s. Little else is known about the community.

OAK LAKE CUT

1872 - 1874

CLASS A

APPROXIMATE LOCATION:
5 Miles east of Audubon on County Highway 144

As railroad crews worked in the area, a headquarters and supply center was established at the site of a big cut in the ridge that separated the waters of the Otter Tail and the Buffalo rivers. The settlement was referred to as a "canvas affair" because it could be taken down and moved to another location within a day. The location was never thought of in terms of longevity. Even though temporary, the settlement included three hotels, three stores, a drug store, meat market, law office, blacksmith, a regional land office and a few other staples.

Railroad officials negotiated for the land to put a more permanent town site at the location but talks stalled when some land owners refused all terms. Knowing there was plenty of land in the area available at a price they were willing to pay, negotiations went forward in nearby locations. The land office was moved to Detroit Lakes and the railroad moved their station to nearby Audubon. By 1872, Oak Lake, or Oak Lake Cut as it was known, was abandoned.

SNELLMAN

1912 – 1919

CLASS D

APPROXIMATE LOCATION:
Just west of the Smoky Hills State Forest, near the intersection of County Highway 34 and 470th Avenue

Back in 1982, Laurie Saarinen represented Park Rapids in the Miss Minnesota pageant. Park Rapids encompassed the rural community of Snellman, where Laurie resided. She won the title of Miss Minnesota and continued on to become a semi-finalist in that year's Miss America

Aune's Kuppala. (Courtesy of Connie Henderson)

Old store in Snellman. (Courtesy of Connie Henderson)

Pageant. For years a sign stood at the outskirts of the rural community telling all who drove through town that Snellman was the home of Miss Minnesota 1982.

More of a community, Snellman was settled by Finnish immigrants in the late 1880s. A railroad station was located in the settlement in the early 1900s. A Lutheran Church congregation was formed in 1912 and a church was constructed the following year. Quickly the church became the community hub and a small settlement developed around the Gethsemane Lutheran Church, which was on Highway 34 in Carsonville Township. The community included a creamery, a hardware store and several homes. Another community staple, the Snellman Store was destroyed by fire in 1931 and was rebuilt. It was demolished in the 1940s and the materials were used to build a home. A new store building was constructed, on the original site, in 1949 and operated until the late twentieth century.

The Forest Tavern was another local landmark and was noted for its burgers and beer. Handmade crafts and woven rugs were offered by the owner until ill health forced her retirement. Today a roadside hamlet, Snellman's has Aune's Kauppla (Finnish for "shop"). It is a quaint shop that offers a wide variety of handmade goods, consignment crafts and a few Finnish items as well. It's open Thursdays through Sundays in the summer months. The old store/gas station still exists and is active and has an occasional yard sale. The Church still stands on the nearby hillside.

TWO INLETS

1900 - 1909

CLASS D

APPROXIMATE LOCATION:
557** County Highway 44, County Road #44 and County #127

After traveling to France and visiting Lourdes, Father Joseph Moylan, of St. Mary's Catholic Church in Two Inlets, Minnesota, was inspired to create a replica of the Lourde's Grotto. With support of the parishioners, in prayer and donations, construction began in 1959. The tree-covered parcel of church land along County Highway #44 near Park Rapids, was the ideal setting. Quiet, serene and reflective, it became even more so with the completion of the Grotto. According to the church website and history, the life-sized statues of Our Lady of Lourdes and St. Bernadette were sculpted of bianeo cairara marble by a renowned Italian artist.

In 1981, Father Alto Butkowski, then pastor of St. Mary's proposed expanding the grotto to include an outdoor Rosary shrine with Stations of the Cross. The shrine is a large rosary designed as a living rosary and was dedicated that same year. Today the Grotto and Stations are every bit as serene and as scenic and still ideal for reflection and prayer. Masses are held at the Grotto during the summer months and for special events.

The area's earliest settlers, in 1891 to 1894, were Catholics who had come from Perham. In the beginning a visiting priest from Aitkin came and offered Mass once a month. Late on, an old barn in Arago Township was converted and used as the first church building until Two Inlets' first church was built in 1903. The parish was considered a mission church of Park Rapids.

Ten years later, in 1913, lightning struck the church and it burned to the ground. In 1914, a second and larger church was built. A parish house followed in 1920 and a parish hall in 1921. On Christmas Eve in 1933, that church also burned to the ground. The resilient parishioners renovated the parish hall and used it for church services until a new church could be constructed. Fittingly the new church building had two entrances, just as there are two inlets on the nearby lake for which the community and township were named.

Just across the road from the church stands the Two Inlets Store. More than a convenience store, the historic business offers an eclectic mix of goods and is a destination for area residents and summer visitors. In speaking with the current owner and a past owner, I learned that the store was built in 1946 and the area was busy and thriving. The village was at one time home to a flour mill and sawmill (which still operates). Today the store invites everyone to stop in, the church is active and thriving and the Grotto and the Stations of the Cross offer respite and reflection. A nearby state park and forestland and the area's many lakes offer recreational opportunities for everyone, thus Two Inlets is still thriving.

Two Inlets Stations of the Cross. (Author's collection)

Statue of St. Bernadette. (Author's collection)

VOSS

1896 - 1907

CLASS A

APPROXIMATE LOCATION:
Border of Walworth and Atlanta Townships Becker County

A devastating tornado wreaked havoc in Becker County in 1902. The swath of the storm was one and one-half miles wide and traveled thirty to fifty miles. Early news reports that a Voss area woman was killed by falling timbers, and four children were killed when their house collapsed. Over thirty buildings and more than $100,000 in damages were incurred.

The small Norwegian community had a post office from 1896 until 1907. The village also included a general store with a telephone exchange from Ulen and Lake Park, a creamery, a cheese factory, restaurant, feed mill, blacksmith, and a community hall.

Voss was the social center of the region with events year-around. Two of the biggest were the annual Fourth of July celebration and the Christmas program. Two area bands provided entertainment and music. Little is known about the demise of the community. Local history books state simply that "Voss is no more."

Two Inlets church. (Author's collection)

Beltrami County

Aure Immanuel Cemetery. (Courtesy of T. Kremer)

Aure vicinity. (Courtesy of T. Kremer)

AURE

1903 – 1919 (1980s)

CLASS C

APPROXIMATE LOCATION:
Intersection of Highways #5 and #24

It is still called Aure Corners, even though nothing remains at the site. The once busy and thriving early 1900s community was located at the intersection of Highways #5 and #24, which was the hub of the town.

At the turn of the twentieth century, Aure was booming. In 1902, the Aure Store opened and continued to operate until 1955 when the land was sold to the Aure Telephone Company. Living quarters were on the side of the store. Always a gathering place for the area, a post office operated from 1903 until 1919 when it was discontinued.

A church was constructed in 1903. The Aure Church was also known as the Norway Lutheran Synod. The sixteen-by-twenty-four-by-ten-foot building was constructed on three donated acres. Services were held about twenty times a year and were conducted in Norwegian, with every third meeting in English. A long wood stove heated the building and kitchen chairs were used for seating. Sometime after 1921 a basement was added, the roof was raised and two additions were added, on each side. The building burned to the ground in 1935. A new church was built in 1937 and electricity was added in

Aure vicinity. (Courtesy of T. Kremer)

1947. When the church merged with the Debs Church, the building was sold and used as a home in Buzzle Township.

The community also had a school. Established in 1903, the first school had a dirt floor and had a term from October to December because the building was just too cold to hold classes the rest of the winter. In the early years, most students spoke only Norwegian. All records of the school were lost. According to a township history booklet compiled and published by the Debs Daily Doers Homemakers Club, the Christmas programs, plays, basket and pie socials, and an annual spring picnic were popular and well-attended. The last school term was in 1944. Early teacher Donna Love recalled that a large wood stove heated the school. A two-foot long log had to be added to the fire every hour on the hour. The school consolidated with Debs in 1944.

Perhaps the most enduring business was the Aure Telephone Company. Established in 1916, there were ninety-three members (Alaska, Buzzle and Roosevelt townships). As the township book details, farmers put up lines between farms so they could call each other. There was no central switchboard so it was not possible to call from one community to another.

The first phones were a rectangular wooden box on the wall with a mouthpiece you spoke into and a receiver for hearing. Two batteries inside provided power. In 1955 an automatic switchboard and long-distance dialing were added. In 1976, the cooperative was sold to the Paul Bunyan Rural Telephone Company.

Several community organizations were active in addition to the Debs Daily Doers among them the Active Ants 4-H club, which began in 1933 and was reactivated in 1952.

By 1998, no buildings remained at the intersection of Highways #5 and #24. A highway sign points the way and the area has a rural population. Aure continues to live in memory.

DEBS

1916 – 1925 (1960s)

CLASS A

APPROXIMATE LOCATION:
Just west of County Road #5 and Debs Road

Five times the presidential candidate for the Socialist Party in the early 1900s, Eugene Debs was especially popular in northern Minnesota, particularly Beltrami County.

Debs District #132 School. (Courtesy of T. Kremer)

The 1912 Presidential Election pitted Woodrow Wilson, Theodore Roosevelt, William Howard Taft, and Eugene V. Debs against each other in the hotly contested race. Election results show that, nationwide, Debs received six-percent of the vote. In Beltrami County he was the top choice. An area group of men formed a Socialist Club and organized a town, which they called Debs. The community was slated to be called Lund, but on the post office application, Lund was scratched out and Debs written in. In Minnesota, there is a township also named for Debs—Eugene in Lake of the Woods County. Nationally there are breweries in Chicago and Michigan and neighborhoods in New York City named for the perennial candidate.

Primarily a logging boom town, the small community included a general store, creamery, post office, auto repair garage, clothing shop, school, and a baseball team. Supplies for the store were transported to Pinewood by railroad, and were then carried by a Model T truck with a wood cab to Debs. The community is said to have close economic ties with nearby Aure.

The first school was held in the "pest" house, so named because it had been used as an infirmary for a nearby logging camp. In 1914 a new school building was constructed. The Aure School and Debs school consolidated in later years.

Community organizations and events were common and popular. Groups included the Farmer's Co-op Club and the Hot Dog Club. Active during 1942 through 1947, the Hot Dog Club was a group of area young people. With gas being rationed, the young folks gathered at local homes on Saturday nights. Since hot dogs were often served, the group became known as the "Hot Dog Club."

The town's heyday was in the 1920s and 1930s. Slowing declining, in 1998 the only remaining business was a gas station/grocery store/restaurant. I'm told Debs has a parade each summer and all are welcome to participate, walk, drive a tractor or whatever they like.

ISLAND LAKE

1906 - 1922

CLASS A

APPROXIMATE LOCATION:
Near intersection of Beltrami County Roads #89 and #32

Railroad, logging, and alcohol played an important role in the history of Island Lake. The village was located on the Crookston Lumber Company's Wilton Spur.

School house at Island Lake, 1905. (Courtesy of Beltrami County Historical Society)

The rail line's primary purpose was to transport logs to a mill in Bemidji. A five-hundred-foot trestle was on the southeast corner of the lake.

With over two hundred loggers in the area during logging time, the settlement included two stores, a hotel, restaurant, school house, jail, sawmill, and at least three saloons. It is said that the saloons were kept busy especially during logging times.

Records tell that the three saloons paid license fees of $700.00 a year and at one time were the village's only source of revenue.

The fast flowing liquor caused multiple problems for the community and logging owners. In March of 1906, a newspaper article stated that authorities "closed" the town. According to the article, the village marshal notified all saloon owners to close their establishments down at 11:00 P.M. on Saturday night and keep them closed all day Sunday. The tactics were required as it was impossible to keep the men sober. Drawing their pay on Saturdays, the men walked to town, cashed their pay vouchers and drank and partied to such extremes they weren't fit to work again until Tuesday. At first, the timber owners tried to limit the excess by only cashing pay vouchers at Fowlds. The loss of sale was so abrupt and total that they tried the tactic of closing the bars from Saturday night and Sunday.

Further problems plagued Island Lake and in 1914, a *Bemidji Pioneer* article stated "Island Lake Ceases to Exist as a Village." The article detailed that a judge filed an order confirming that the incorporation of Island Lake was fraudulent and illegal and ordered the village to cease.

The village, less than fifteen acres in size, included part of the Red Lake Indian Reservation. At its peak the platted

Island Lake today. (Courtesy of T. Kremer)

portion had nineteen residents (down to five adults and seven children in 1914). It never had more than eight buildings (down to five with one vacant). The town's only revenue was from saloon licenses. The article noted that all of the lands were wild, uncultured and uninhabitable. Analysts theorize that the real reason for the suit was to prevent the granting of liquor licenses and the maintenance of a saloon in an isolated place next to the Indian reservation.

Later news reports state simply that the Village of Island Lake disappeared. A highway sign still marks the location of the village.

JELLE

1903 - 1938

CLASS A

APPROXIMATE LOCATION:
Hamre Township, On County Road #707, two miles south of intersection of #700 and #707

Determining that it was just too cold to stop his horses at all of the mailboxes on the route, the Jelle postmaster decided to wait until spring to deliver the mail. Postal authorities had received complaints that first class mail was being lost and not delivered. A U.S. postal inspector was sent to investigate. He found that a letter sent from Jelle to Thorhult, a distance of seven miles had not been delivered on schedule. Investigating further, the inspector visited the home of the postmaster, where he found stacks of undelivered mail. That was when the postmaster informed the investigator of his warmer weather delivery plans. The postmaster was promptly dishonorably discharged. Little else is known about the community.

MALCOLM

1904 - 1944

CLASS C

APPROXIMATE LOCATION:
Beltrami County #18 and County #703 (Malcolm Road NW)

The early Swedish settlers chose to name their new community after their homeland in Vaarmeland, Sweden. The Swedish spelling was Malkolm but the postal service recorded it with the English spelling, Malcolm.

Little is known about the community. Records tell that the area was beset by natural disasters in the early 1900s. A fire in 1917 was followed two year later by a flood that left the countryside underwater for weeks. In 1931 a second fire destroyed several buildings as well as including some fatalities.

A post office operated from 1904 until 1944.

NEBISH

1898 - 1963

CLASS C

APPROXIMATE LOCATION:
7 miles north of Buena Vista on Beltrami County #15, near the junction of #15 and #32

Truly a lumber and railroad location, Nebish was an original stop on the Red Lake line, which later became the Minneapolis, Redby, Manitoba Railroad. In the late 1800s, lumbermen had contracts with the Crookston Lumber Company to log the region and in 1895, the Arpin brothers set up a logging camp. A narrow gauge railroad ran from Nebish Lake to the Lower Red Lake and had spurs to the camps. A settlement grew around the original stop and was called Nebish, after the Ojibwe name for tea, "anibish." In 1898 a post office was established and had two hundred patrons. It was housed in the general store. Rather long-lived the post office operated until 1959 and then as a rural branch until 1963.

A Catholic Church, Saint's Peter and Paul was established in the early 1920s. The church's name was later changed to

Nebish School, 1900. (Courtesy of Beltrami County Historical Society)

St. John's. The community also had a school that operated until the 1960s when it consolidated with Blackduck. In 1998, the school was the only major structure from the village's hey-day still standing.

Baseball was extremely popular, and Nebish had a town team from the 1920s until the 1940s. The 1940s signaled a significant decline in Nebish. The Red Lake line stopped running in 1932 and the tracks were pulled up in 1939. Left to nature it was assumed the grade would rapidly deteriorate and be reclaimed by nature but it stayed in good shape. In 1956, Beltrami County acquired the right of way and used the grade for the roadbed of the new Highway 15. Today a few homes, the church and the community name remain.

ROSBY

Early 1900s

CLASS A/G

APPROXIMATE LOCATION:
Near intersection of U.S. #2 and County Highway #4

Pumping gas in the early days of auto travel was a bit different than it is today. The tall pumps were hand operated. The top part was glass and the station attendant would pump gas into the glass top, which was marked off in gallons. Once the purchased amount was pumped into the glass top, the station attendant would then put a hose (similar to today's) and pump it into the car's gas tank.

Rosby had two grocery stores, each with a gas pump, one a Red Crown brand, the other Standard Oil. The community was named for Ole Rosby, one of the Great Northern Railroad's surveying crew members. A creamery was also part of the community. One former resident recalled that buttermilk sold for ten cents per five-gallon bucket. While some drank the buttermilk,

it was often used a hog feed. Potatoes were the cash crop and were shipped out by the train car load. Rosby declined with improved transportation and less dependence on the railroad.

Early gas pumps. (Author's collection)

Rosby Creamery picnic. (Courtesy of Beltrami County Historical Society)

Rosby Today. (Courtesy of T. Kremer)

SAUM

1904 - 1944

CLASS C

APPROXIMATE LOCATION:
Highway #23 (Pioneer Road NE) just north of
Tolgen Road NE

Celebrating one hundred years in 1912, the Saum School is truly a historic site. Listed on the National Register of Historic Places, the community and history-minded people of the Saum area, past and present, keep the history of the school and the community alive. There is even a Facebook page detailing the efforts, events, and goings on at the school.

The school lays claim to a historic first. It was the first consolidated school in Minnesota, only the third in the entire United States. In 1912, three area school districts consoli-

dated. The two-story building housed both elementary and high school grades. Initially the enrollment was over 100 students. By 1960, when the school closed only twenty-five students attended.

The very first Saum School was a one-room log building, which still stands next to the two-story building. Too far for

Original Saum school, 1903-1912. (Courtesy of T. Kremer)

32

Saum School. (Author's collection)

most students to walk, the school district provided transportation via a horse-drawn wagon or sleigh. Now owned by the Beltrami Historical Society, the two school buildings host events and are open to tourists and visitors.

Saum's first settler was Ole Vang who came to the region in 1901. In those days, water was the only means of transportation. Settlers had to first come by Red Lake and Battle River. In 1903, access by rail was available.

A post office was established in 1904 and the name "Saum" was chosen because it was the shortest name submitted. Mail came three times a week, first from Battle River and later Kelliher. All freight and merchandise came by way of Kelliher, thirteen miles away. During the summer and wet seasons that trip took two to three days. The post office was discontinued in 1944. Though most of the town lives in memory and history, the Saum School has an active preservation society. Reunions, special events, and other activities take place year-round.

Saum store and post office, 1913. (Courtesy of Beltrami County Historical Society)

Wilderness store, Saum. (Courtesy of T. Kremer)

Saum outhouse. (Courtesy of the Saum Historic School Facebook page)

SHILLING

1917 - 1935

CLASS A

APPROXIMATE LOCATION:
Approximate location only within Beltrami Game Reserve

Shilling's early mail carrier had a unique method of delivering the mail. He loaded the sack of mail on the back of his horse, then hitched a pair of skis to the horse and off they would go, through sleet and snow, to deliver the mail.

Little is known about the community. It did have post office (named for the store keeper) from 1917 until 1935. It also had a store and school. It is now part of the recreational land reserves of Beltrami County.

SHOOKS

1911 – 1966

CLASS D

APPROXIMATE LOCATION:
Intersection of Minnesota Highways #1 and #72

I just knew from driving Highway #72 and turning at Highway #1 that the area had once been a busy settlement. Several buildings still stand: the church, a town hall/school and old store/bait shop/gas station, and the still operating Shooks Motel.

In 1892, the Crookston Lumber Company was operating in the area. In 1903, the Minneapolis and International Railroad had a loading station at the location. Soon there was a hotel, depot, mercantile, school, town hall and a church. A post office operated for over fifty years, from 1911 until 1966. The railroad stopped services in 1966.

People from all over the region remember the Shooks store and gas station, which did continue to operate for years, lastly, in recent times, being a bait store, convenience goods and gas. The pumps and the old signage remain.

Shooks church. (Author's collection)

Above: Two views of Shooks Bait and Gas. (Author's collection)

Shooks postcard. (Author's collection)

Shooks. (Author's collection)

Spaulding

1897 - 1908

CLASS A

APPROXIMATE LOCATION:
Highway 28 just east of 360th Avenue

Spaulding's post office was short-lived but had many homes. As each new postmaster took office, the post office moved to their residence or business. The community, primarily a logging community with the sawmill the major industry, was named for an early logger. The community had two schools, the East and the West. The first church services were in 1906. Little else is known.

Thorhult

1906 - 1935

CLASS A

APPROXIMATE LOCATION:
Near junction of Beltrami County #42 (Thorhult Road NW)
and Minnesota #89

Students at the Sandridge or Thorhult School in Thorhult made a deal with their teacher. If she would let them "go sliding" at lunch time, they would race back to school when the bell rang. If tardy, they wouldn't be allowed to "go sliding" the next day.

The only hill large enough to slide down was a sawdust pile. According to Genevieve Sjorey Helgenson, who was a student at the school from 1919 to 1926, she recalled that the students carried pails of water to make the hill slippery. Then at noon they took their homemade slides and went sliding down the sawdust pile now covered in ice.

A post office operated in the community from 1906 to 1935.

OTHER BELTRAMI COUNTY TOWNS

Most of these towns were covered in *Minnesota's Lost Towns: Northern Edition*. Since that time, we have added these photos.

Foy Tabernacle. (Courtesy of T. Kremer)

Quiring town hall. (Courtesy of T. Kremer)

Bartin post office site. (Courtesy of T. Kremer)

Bartin school site. (Courtesy of T. Kremer)

Foy cemetery. (Courtesy of T. Kremer)

Beltrami County #33, Shotley. (Courtesy of T. Kremer)

Domaas. (Courtesy of T. Kremer)

Domaas Upper Red Lake. (Courtesy of T. Kremer)

Fowlds site. (Courtesy of T. Kremer)

Foy Road. (Courtesy of T. Kremer)

Fowlds site. (Courtesy of T. Kremer)

Cass County

Cuba Hill Fire Tower. (Courtesy of T. Kremer)

Schley ranger station. (Courtesy of National Archives Collection)

Cuba Hill guard station. (Courtesy of National Archives Collection)

Chain O'Lakes Resort, Schley. (Author's collection)

Cuba/Santiago/Schley

1898 - 1968

CLASS A/C

APPROXIMATE LOCATION:
Along U.S. Highway 2 East of Cass Lake

Not only were the three communities in close proximity, all three were settled in 1898 to 1899, and were also were successive stations along the Great Northern Railroad Line east of Cass Lake. All three were named in commemoration of the Spanish American War.

Cuba and Santiago were named after the site of a decisive naval battle against Spain. Little is known about either town. Cuba's station was built in 1899 and was abandoned in the late 1920s. Santiago's depot was also built in 1899 and was abandoned in 1914. Finding any trace of Santiago has proven unsuccessful. Cuba does have a standing fire tower on Cuba Hill and it overlooks the area.

Schley had a longer life span than both Cuba and Santiago. Schley was named in honor of U.S. Naval Admiral Winfield Scott Schley. Schley commanded the "Flying Squadron" during the Spanish American War at Santiago, Cuba. Also established on the Great Northern Railroad line from Duluth to Cass Lake, it was also later abandoned. In 1910, when the Soo Line Railroad established a line from Federal Dam to Plummer, Schley began its second existence. The rail station was discontinued in 1956, yet Schley lived on. Its post office operated from 1931 until 1968. There are some tourist cabins and some original buildings in the area.

Leader

1903 - 1960s

CLASS D

APPROXIMATE LOCATION:
12 Miles North of Motley on Highway 64

Creameries were often the foundation of a town's creation and its basis for survival, and they often outlived other aspects of a town. There were especially important in so-called "inland towns," towns many miles from railroad service. Leader, in southern Cass County was one of those inland towns being fifteen miles from the nearest rail service and the creamery was the town's mainstay.

Said to be Cass County's largest creamery, Leader's creamery, known as the Swan Valley Creamery, was built in 1901. The creamery was busy six days a week. Monday, Wednesday, and Friday were called "cream days." An anonymously authored history of the community on file at the Cass County Historical Society states that those three days were when the farmers brought their cream to town. Tuesdays, Thursdays, and Saturdays were the days when the cream was churned into butter. Cream days were so busy residents had a hard time finding parking.

A 1925 article in *The Walker Pilot* writes of the benefits of having a creamery in town. As the reporter surmised, a creamery was a strong magnet as it brought farmers to town. If they were able to do their shopping at the same time, "it is killing two birds with one stone."

In 1910, the original creamery building was destroyed by fire, supposedly one in the smoke stack. Farmers raced to fight the fire, but the building was beyond rescue, so the men tried to save

Leader's vintage display. (Author's collection)

Leader Rocks. (Author's collection)

Leader's Elvis. (Author's collection)

the contents, but only a few tubs of butter were salvaged. A $1,400.00 insurance policy didn't cover the $3,000.00 in damages. Realizing the importance of the creamery to the community, volunteers donated their labor and time to rebuild the structure. Construction was begun almost immediately.

A general store was instrumental to the community as well. *The Walker Pilot* also stated that the store, located some fifteen miles from rail service had to have a larger inventory than one located close to supply lines. Leader also had a post office which lasted from the early twentieth century, closing in the 1960s. Also included in the community were a second store (later a saddle and harness shop), a garage and machine shop along Highway 64, an auto garage, and a blacksmith/welding shop. A tavern was built in the 1930s. Originally known as

"Haag," it is now the "Bear's Den." A unique attraction is the Bear's Den's pig races. Held most Friday and Saturday nights during the warm months, the races are kid-friendly and family-oriented. The Bear's Den also hosts Growler Days, an all-day event that features a parade, food, horseshoes, kid's events, bear growling contest, pig races, and fireworks.

Elvis Presley and Marilyn Monroe are also represented in today's Leader. On display in the convenience store/gas station, they are joined by other 1950s era décor. Two churches, both from nearby lost towns (Ellis and Esterdy) were moved to Leader and are still active. The Leader School, first built in 1941 was moved and torn down when Leader students began to go to school in Motley.

The Leader Lions Community Club began with the Woodmen's Lodge of Leader. When that hall burned, a small insurance fund and donations were received for the construction of a new hall, one mile north of Leader. Completed in 1946, dances were hosted to help pay off the building debt.

Leader sure sounds like a busy place for a long-ago town, and that it is. The post office is gone as is the town structure. Yet Leader is still filled with community spirit and pride, as it has always been.

OSHAWA
1916 - 1944 (1970s)
CLASS C
APPROXIMATE LOCATION:
Eight miles west of Backus on Highway 87

Each town, every community, even rural communities have that one place that gives it heart. It is the place everyone remembers fondly. For the rural Cass County community of Oshawa, it was the Oshawa Store. From all accounts the combination store/post office, and later gas station and tavern, was the epitome of an old-fashioned country store. The multi-purpose store sold everything area residents could need. You could get your supplies, check your mail, send packages, get a money order, gas up the auto, get liquid refreshments and catch up on all the news. It was the heart and soul of the region.

Built in 1915 by the Lutien family, the store and locality were named after the Lutien's former home of Oshawa, Ontario, Canada. In 1916, a post office was added and operated until 1944. Mail carriers would stop twice a day to get stamps cancelled and make out money orders.

Oshawa store today. (Courtesy of A. Filer)

45

Oshawa area today. (Courtesy of A. Filer)

In 1931, the original store building burned to the ground. The local newspapers reported the cause of the fire was a short circuit in a small electrical light plant that ignited spilled gasoline. Within a half-hour, the wood building was in ashes. It was rebuilt that same year.

Tragedy struck the small community in 1936, when the store owner died in an early, heavy snowstorm. The young man, in his early forties and of the Lutien family, had been suffering from ill health, a heart condition. Apparently his car stalled in the storm, and he was unable to get it going again. A local newspaper account writes that he took off on foot. Tracks told the story of his journey and his untimely death. Walking towards a nearby farm house, he must have become disoriented and confused. Falling into a ditch, it appeared he crawled on his hands and knees for a bit eventually succumbing to the elements and his bad heart.

Betty Zaffke fondly remembers the store. In 1991, she wrote her memoirs. She also shared her memories with me in the summer of 2014. Tom Holden, another area resident, also shared his memories with me. Both recalled that the store sold a wide variety of items, everything from bolts of fabric to nuts and bolts to grocery goods. The store carried a wide variety of goods, there just wasn't much choice in each category.

Most grocery items were sold in bulk, including crackers, cookies, flour, sugar, and more. The primary brand was Monarch, as that was the supplier's (Nash Finch's) brand. Fresh meat was available during the cold months. Betty recalls that every now and then Nash Finch would bring ice cream, wrapped in canvas. Word got out quickly and area residents rushed to the store to get some before it melted.

The store owners purchased eggs, cream, homemade butter, and logs from area residents. The cream was shipped to Duluth. During hard times, the store owners let customers charge their purchases, paying when they could, if they could. During the 1950s into the 1970s, the store operated as a "beer joint."

Today the building stills stands and is now a summer residence. The store community may be gone, but it lives on in the hearts of many former residents.

PONTORIA

1903 - 1919

CLASS C

APPROXIMATE LOCATION:
12½ Miles South of Longville on Highway 84

Highway 84 is a winding country road that traverses some of the most scenic landscapes, especially in the fall color season. Along the route to Longville stands a white building with a store front that looks like the old store fronts of yore. The building, constructed in 1923, still stands and is used as a family residence.

A former resident recalls that the store was in three different locations along the shores of Ponto Lake in Ponto Lake Township. The first sites may have been a Wells-Fargo stage stop. Little else is known about the community, which today is a summer vacation haven.

RICHARDS
Early 1900s
CLASS A/F
APPROXIMATE LOCATION:
Highway 2 West of Bena on Forest Road 2074 for one mile,
on shores of Lake Winnibigoshish

Folks still pitch tents at the Richards town site, just as they did over one hundred years ago. Back then, they were trying to establish a town site. Today, the site is home to the Richards Town Site Campground on the shores of Lake Winnibigoshish in the Chippewa National Forest in Cass County.

Town site organizers had big plans for their proposed settlement. The group looked at several timber-rich areas along the Great Northern Railroad line. Selecting three hundred acres just west of another proposed town site, Bena, they knew that was the location they wanted. The acreage, located within the confines of the Chippewa Indian Reservation, carried special conditions required of a new town site by a law passed by Congress for new town sites within reservations.

The town site people set up tents on their chosen location. They named the new development, Richards, in honor of the commissioner of the General Land Office in Washington, D.C. For a short while, the town had a drug store, and a newspaper, *The Richards Record*. The Natives did not like the idea of the new village or thought of losing the valuable timber land. They complained to the area's Indian agent, who in turn, ordered the town site development group off the land. Ignoring the order, the group began building small homes and other buildings. They were promptly arrested as trespassers.

A legal battle ensued between the General Land Office and the Department of the Interior. Complicating matters further was the fact that a new town site was petitioned for just a mile from Richards, that being Bena. As a result, the Richards town site claim was rejected on the grounds that the organizers had not completed the application as specified by the requirements of the newly passed town site law. The legal battle lasted over three years. The court's decision set a precedent for town site creation and development. The Richards people purchased land two miles west of the proposed town site and all the Richard's buildings were moved there. Today, a historical marker stands at the original town site location.

Richards town site. (Courtesy of T. Kremer)

Richards town site. (Courtesy of T. Kremer)

Crow Wing County

Gorst's Mill/Gorstville

1880 – 1900s

CLASS B

APPROXIMATE LOCATION:
4 miles northeast of Camp Ripley on U.S. #371, across the road from Pine Grove Cemetery on the South side of the river

Lasting only as long as the region's timber lasted, Gorst's Mill/Gorstville still had visible remains one hundred years later. In 1880, John Gorst built a sawmill along the Little Nokassippi River four miles northeast of Camp Ripley. A small community grew up around the mill and in part included the mill and a collection of houses and a school. The school, one-quarter mile from the settlement was known as District #6, the Troxell School. Plans were made to consolidate with District #16 in 1913 but the building burned to the ground before the consolidation took effect.

When the timber supply was gone, the mill moved and with it most of the settlers, abandoning the church and other buildings. The church had been active for years. Later a Catholic Church was established at nearby St. Mathias.

Nearly a century later, in 1978, a Minnesota Archeology Site study was conducted. The study found building depressions, dam remains, and the remains of an old bridge. In 1987 another study stated the remains of a log dam were found in the river directly below the dam remains as well as large logs and planks considered to be the remnants of the sawmill. Anchor bolts still attached to wooden beams were found buried in the ground high on the bank. Remains of an old road could be seen fifty feet downstream from the 1987 bridge.

Grant County

Erdahl's main street today. (Author's collection)

Erdahl raiway station. (Courtesy of the Grant County Historical Society)

ERDAHL

1887 - 1980s

CLASS D

APPROXIMATE LOCATION:
8 Miles east of Elbow Lake on County Highway #79

Once a thriving trade center along the Great Northern Railroad's branch line from Evansville to Tintah, Erdahl was home to over fifteen businesses. The community, platted in Erdahl Township in 1887 during its heyday included: a grocery and confectionary store, grain elevator, telephone cooperative, blacksmith shop, implement dealer, hardware, general store, creamery, bank, lumberyard, sawmill, garage and filling station, restaurant, barber shop, pool hall, butcher shop, post office, train depot, a church, and a school. While some were short-lived, a few lasted for decades.

A post office began in 1883 and operated until 1954. For a short time, from 1890 to 1891 the town was known as "Cork." The name was bantered about by workers unloading a train car of cork beer barrels, and the name stuck for a year or so.

Clearing land was a never ending chore for the area's farmers in the 1890s. One day, in 1894, while removing stumps from his field, a farmer came upon a battle ax buried six inches under a stump. It was unlike any he had seen so he decided to have it checked out. The initial resource dated the ax to the fourteenth century. The find was so special that, for a while, in 1964, it was in the possession of the Crown Prince of Norway. Later metal tests proved the ax to be of French origin from the seventeenth century. It is assumed that a French guide or Red River Oxcart driver lost it between 1830 and 1860. It is now on display at the Runestone Museum in Alexandria, Minnesota.

In 1902, a one-room school was built, but, due to the large number of students, a second room and another teacher were added in 1929. Both rooms were used until 1943. In 1951, the school consolidated with the Elbow Lake School system. Grades one through six were taught in the building until 1953 at which time the school was closed.

One of the longest lasting elements of the town was the Erdahl Lutheran Church. Formed by the merger of the Bethel Norsk Evangelical Menighad Church and the Pomme de Terre Norsk Evangelical Church, the church was active for over 100 years. Closed in 2005, the building was sold and it became a private home and artist's studio. After that it sat empty for a few years and was purchased in early 2014 and at that time was an archery shooting range.

Community organizations hosted several events and worked to promote and improve life in Erdahl. The Erdahl Farmer's Club, active during the early 1900s fostered educational and social activities. Meeting at least once a month, a variety of events including music, lectures, programs and were always capped with a lunch. The area's Community Club hosted an annual day-long picnic with music, recitations, games and food. The Erdahl Improvement Company's mission was to make Erdahl the best place in Grant County to do your business.

Erdahl was hit hard during the Great Depression of the 1930s. Several businesses closed as did the bank. The elevator was sold and was slated to move seven miles to Evansville. It broke apart even before it was on the road. Many farmers sold out during World War II.

After the bank closed in 1932, the Kjelstrup family purchased the building and started a restaurant in 1934. Operating for over fifty years, the restaurant was a popular spot for

Erdahl Restaurant. (Courtesy of the Grant County Historical Society)

Early Erdahl's main street. (Courtesy of the Grant County Historical Society)

residents, travelers, tourists and the area's visiting hunters and fishers. During the 1940s and 1950s, dances were held at the Erdahl Town Hall, located just behind the restaurant. The owners tell that over forty pounds of hamburger was cooked and eaten during the dances as the 200 patrons moved easily from one building to the other. The café closed in 1986 when Aggie Kjelstrup, the owner, retired.

Today the only business in the roadside hamlet is a well driller. The creamery still stands, as does the church, bank/restaurant and the Town Hall. A friendly, inviting park is at the edge of town.

Erdah's former restaurant and bank today. (Courtesy of the Grant County Historical Society

Erdah's former restaurant and bank today. (Author's collection)

Restaurant entry today. (Author's collection)

Erdah's township hall today. (Author's collection)

56

Hubbard County

White Oak Bible Chapel, Chamberlain. (Author's collection)

White Oak Town Hall, Chamberlain. (Author's collection)

Guthrie garage. (Courtesy of T. Kremer)

Guthrie 2014. (Courtesy of T. Kremer)

CHAMBERLAIN

1898 -1916

CLASS D

APPROXIMATE LOCATION:
Minnesota Highway #64 and Hubbard County #170th Street

Every time I drive Minnesota Highway #64 to Bemidji, I drive through Chamberlain and wonder what its history is. The White Oak Town Hall, White Oak Chapel, the White Oak Cemetery and a few homes and buildings mark the location. I've asked everyone and researched multiple sources, finding little information. Postal records indicate that the community had a post office from 1898 until 1916.

GUTHRIE

1900 - 1980

CLASS D

APPROXIMATE LOCATION:
6 miles from Laporte off of Minnesota #200

The small Hubbard County community was named for Archibald Guthrie, a contractor for the Minnesota and International Railway. The community had a post office from 1900 until 1980.

Guthrie buildings. (Courtesy of T. Kremer)

HUBBARD

1880 - 1968

CLASS D

APPROXIMATE LOCATION:
Junction of Minnesota #87 and Hubbard County #6

At one time, 1885 to be specific, Hubbard's population of 126 was larger than that of neighboring Park Rapids. Both communities were rivals in the bid for designation of the Hubbard county seat, and in 1886, Hubbard officially petitioned for the seat. Park Rapids won the bid.

Guthrie streets. (Courtesy of T. Kremer)

First called Brighton by the surveyor, the town's settlers preferred Manter. That name lasted a short, then was back to Brighton for two years. Then, in the hopes of winning the county seat prize, it was changed to Hubbard, which it remains. When platted, the north/south streets in Manter were Jefferson, Lake, and Main. Numbered streets (First through Third) ran east/west. First street was on the north side of town. In 1885, two blocks were added to the south side of town and became known as "Todd's addition to Brighton."

Multiple name changes applied not only to the town but to the community's newspapers as well. In 1887 the newspaper was called *The Hubbard Bulletin*, in 1888 it changed to *The Independent Bulletin*, and in 1891, it was back to the original name.

Sticking with the name change theme, the 1882 Manter Hotel later became the Hubbard Hotel and Hubbard House. The Hubbard County Historical Society has the original hotel register from 1886 to 1888 on display. The register shows the signatures of the people who stayed at or ate at the hotel during those years.

Hubbard grew rapidly primarily because of its location on the Hubbard Prairie and the Wheat Trail. The closest grain elevator was at the Northern Pacific Rail station in Verndale, so most of the wheat went through Hubbard and Shell City. After the Great Northern Railroad built from Wadena to Park Rapids in 1891, wheat was hauled to elevators in Latona and Park Rapids. Ultimately, the train and the changed traffic would dictate the demise of Hubbard.

The bustling town was at its busiest in the late nineteenth and early twentieth centuries. In it's heyday, the community included a hardware, millenary, two blacksmiths, a shoe and

Long Lake Theater, Hubbard. (Author's collection)

Hubbard today. (Author's collection)

Hubbard landmark. (Author's collection)

Hubbard streets. (Author's collection)

harness shop, flour mill, dentist, livery, telephone exchange office, a sawmill, three general stores, a bank, and at least two saloons. There had been a creamery in the early days, but it was destroyed by fire and never rebuilt. There was also an Odd Fellows Hall. The hall hosted dances, basket and pie socials, and served as the town hall and meeting place for the Odd Fellows. After the dances ended about midnight, a supper was often furnished. This large two-story building had a stage on the first floor. The second floor had a carpeted lodge room with a kitchen and waiting room. Hubbard County's second school was also in the community.

A thirty-six-by-forty-eight-foot dam was built. It rose nearly three feet above the foundation. Business was brisk and wheat sold for thirty-five cents a bushel. In November of 1885, the dam broke, and the flour mill toppled into the river. It was rebuilt the next year.

The post office, which operated from 1880 until 1968 was robbed in 1897. Explosives were used to blow the safe and the thieves made off with four hundred dollars.

Hubbard had two churches, a Methodist established in 1890 and a Baptist in 1892.

A 1933 news report tells of a severe storm moving through the area. Roofs were blown off and hail as "big as hens eggs" fell.

In the early twenty-first century, a community church was moved a short distance and the Long Lake Theater was established. The 100-seat renovated church/theater is home to several productions throughout the year. All summer long and into the fall, tour buses, cars, and people flock to see the best in area talent and theater. The Hilltop Café has also been a long-standing local landmark. The Hubbard Town Hall is located across the street from the theater. A scenic boat landing and fishing pier round out today's Hubbard.

LATONA

1895 - 1909

CLASS A

APPROXIMATE LOCATION:
North of Menagha at intersection of U.S. Highway #71 and 120th Street

On the surface, the historical records indicated that Latona and Horton were interchangeable, both referring to the same location. While that is true, it

Latona/Horton railway to the north. (Courtesy of T. Kremer)

does require some clarification. Latona was the name of the post office and Horton the name of the rail station. Slightly confusing, the two names are the same community. The name, "Latona" is from mythology. Latona was the wife of Zeus and the mother of Apollo and Artemis.

The settlement was along the Great Northern Railroad line running from Sauk Centre to Cass Lake. An 1891 newspaper article tells of a new town and also tells that fifty lots were

Latona rail line along right of way. (Courtesy of T. Kremer)

begin given away to anyone who would come and establish a building in the new community. Soon the town was thriving and had at least: two stores, two elevators, a large sawmill right in town, a hotel, post office from 1895 to 1909, and the Knowles School, which also served as a church and Sunday school. In 1898 a telephone line was being built from Latona to Park Rapids.

Today the old railroad grade is used by ATV and snowmobile enthusiasts. A home and an attached business were recently on the Latona town site.

Latona/Horton railway to the north. (Courtesy of T. Kremer)

NARY

1899 - 1924

CLASS C

APPROXIMATE LOCATION:
6 Miles south of Bemidji, on Hubbard County #9, one mile east of U.S. #71

Logging was the lure of the region. By 1898, the Minneapolis and International Railroad (later Northern Pacific) had five spurs to area logging camps. Estimates say over 1,000 loggers were in the area. Nary had an official population of 330.

Organized out of Cass County, the township was first called Goshen Land because it was the most valuable land in Hubbard County. When the papers were filed, the name was changed to Helga after the first child born in the township.

Nary was incorporated in 1899 and named for an early sawmill owner, Thomas Nary, also later a county surveyor. Immediately a school district was organized, and plans were made to construct a schoolhouse by January of 1900. Nary's first church services were held in the old school until 1902 when the Baptist Church was built. The school bell for the new building was taken from a Mississippi River steamboat. The bell was later moved to the Baptist Church in 1948 because the church bell was cracked. In 1919 a new school was built. Three years of high school grades were offered in addition to

Nary National Airport, Shefland Field. (Courtesy of T. Kremer)

Nary, 1900. (Courtesy of the Helga Town Board)

Early Nary school. (Courtesy of the Helga Town Board)

Nary school, 1940. (Courtesy of the Helga Town Board)

Nary school children. (Courtesy of the Helga Town Board)

Nary school, 1940. (Courtesy of the Helga Town Board)

the elementary grades. Because there was no state aid for high school courses, the high school grades were discontinued in 1939. The school building defines today's Nary.

With over one-thousand loggers in the area, saloons were a bustling business. Nary had four saloons (some say six), a restaurant, four "big" stores, a post office that operated from 1899 to 1924, a hat shop, blacksmith, and the Smiley Hotel. With multiple saloons a jail was an important and necessary part of the village. There was also a building called the "Big Paul Building." It housed a dance hall, large restaurant, hardware, machine shop, and feed store.

A fire swept through the area, destroying most of Nary in 1901. Most businesses rebuilt. In 1908 another fire swept the region, and only a few buildings survived.

After the decline of logging, area residents tried farming. The land was less than ideal for farming and most could not make a living at it. Early residents recalled that the land had fifty to sixty tree stumps, most more than four feet across, per acre. Many residents supplemented their income by going to the Dakotas and working the harvest.

A town band was organized in 1931 and celebrated its fiftieth anniversary in 1981. The founder and several original band members were with the band for the entire fifty years. There were a few years, during wars, that the band was inactive.

In the 1930s a passenger train ran from Nary to Bemidji. Residents often made the journey for shopping and to take in a movie. Rocks were abundant in the area and one resident decided to stop fighting them and established a rock shop. He made rock tables well into the 1970s.

The Nary School consolidated with the Bemidji Schools in 1969. In 1970, the Guthrie School joined Nary and enrollment was one hundred and twenty students. Because of overcrowding, some students had to be transported to Bemidji, where most went to the new Horace May school just south of Bemidji. The Nary school closed in 1972. A referendum voted down the closure, but since the state took away all state aid, there was no choice but to close the school. For many years, the building sat vacant and deteriorating, subject to the elements and vandals.

Nary from the east. (Courtesy of T. Kremer)

In the 1980s, Helga Township was in need of a new hall and discussion turned to the possibility of using the old school building as a town and community center. The debate was over the option of building a new hall or restoring the old school and repurposing it. Inspections determined that the old school building was structurally sound. A special election was held to decide the matter, and the community began the restoration of the historic building. With much time, effort and work, the community began the restoration. The upstairs of the building had a seventy-two-foot auditorium that stretches the entire length of the building. The town board, area residents, and past residents have undertaken the task of restoring, maintaining and preserving the historic school. Efforts are underway to have the building placed on the National Register of Historic Places. Special events, programs, reunions, picnics, and many other celebrations are held at the school year round. Nary is a true example of the present preserving the past for the future.

YOLA

1903 - 1933

CLASS A

APPROXIMATE LOCATION:
FROM LAKE GEORGE - SOUTHWEST ON US 71 TO COUNTY 4 - TURN RIGHT ON COUNTY 4 FOR 1 MILE - LEFT TO STAY ON COUNTY 4 FOR 2½ MILES (3 miles from Lake George)

Though the post office was established in 1903 and discontinued in 1933, Yola seems to have had no official beginning or ending.

Frank J. Mitchell, Hubbard County historian, writes that Yola was a thriving town as it was located on the shortest,

Lake George Post Office. (Courtesy of T. Kremer)

Yola marker. (Courtesy of T. Kremer)

actually the only road between Park Rapids and Bemidji. The town was named for the first child born in Lake George Township. It had a sawmill, a hotel, with the post office on the first floor and rooms to rent on the second, Later there were several steam-operated lath mills in the town

Lake George, just three miles south of Yola, was a small settlement, but when U.S. Highway #71 was built in 1940, Lake George grew faster. Yola would gradually decline until it no longer existed as a town. The post office was eventually moved to Lake George, where it still stands and is active. At one time it was considered the smallest post office in the United States.

Yola today. (Courtesy of T. Kremer)

Streets of Yola. (Courtesy of T. Kremer)

Itasca County

A day's catch at Lakewood Lodge in the 1920s. (Courtesy of Lakewood Lodge, Inger, Minnesota)

Early fishermen at Lakewood Lodge. (Courtesy of Lakewood Lodge, Inger, Minnesota)

ACROPOLIS

1892 - 1930

CLASS A/G

APPROXIMATE LOCATION:
Just north of Goodland and part of Goodland since the 1930s

Logging and farming were the main occupations in the area. With the Wright and Davis Logging Railroad having a route through the community, Acropolis was established as an election district for the nearby camps, including the Swan River Logging Company. The area's Greek workers named the community, Acropolis, in honor of their homeland.

In 1893 a water tower was built and in 1899 the Great Northern Railroad added a telegraph office. The area was home to many farms, including the very large Fowler Farm (which consisted of forty parcels of forty acres each). To accommodate those farms, the railroad built a depot in 1918. The depot was a ten-by-fourteen-foot rail car, and it had no agent. Townspeople often used it as a warming house. In 1918, a wood-frame school was also built.

The most vivid memories of early settlers were the howling wolves and the hungry mosquitoes.

Acropolis merged into the Goodland community in the 1930s.

BLACKBERRY

1899 - 1944

CLASS A/G

APPROXIMATE LOCATION:
U.S. Highway #2 Itasca County Road #71, 7 miles SE of Grand Rapids

Playing a key role in the region's development, the Mississippi River bisects Blackberry Township. A river boat landing, near the present Blackberry Bridge, was the primary means of transportation until the Duluth and Winnipeg Railroad came to the region in 1889. At one time, the area was thick with blackberry bushes, thus the name of the village and the township.

Settled by Scandinavian immigrants, the area's primary activities were logging and farming. Potatoes were a cash crop and often supplemented farm incomes. Timber resources were nearly depleted by 1916, though farmers continued to harvest poplar for many years. Timber has also rebounded through the years.

The first store was a log building built in 1899. A school building was constructed in 1894, a new depot with a 100-foot loading platform was built in 1906. Several community groups were ac-

tive, including a Farmer's Club in 1915 and a Ladies Social Club. A post office operated from 1899 until 1944. Baseball was a popular pastime, and Blackberry's team was said to be very good.

Blackberry's close proximity to Grand Rapids would prove to be the chief cause of its decline. As transportation improved, Blackberry residents were able to travel to Grand Rapids stores and businesses. Within a short time Blackberry lost its post office, feed store, and railroad amenities. The name, however, does live on in the township and the region.

BRUCE SIDING

1900 - 1920 (1940)

CLASS A

APPROXIMATE LOCATION:
Between Swan River and Goodland (3 miles north of Swan River)

Train engineers dreaded Bruce Hill. With a grade of 1.57 percent, the hill was so steep, trains would stall out. They would then have to back down the hill all the way to Swan River and have to try again to make it over the hill.

Home to the A.C. Bruce Lumber Company, the siding was cut off from a large area of forest by a parcel of private land. The landowner was upset over the Bruce Company trespassing on his property and even cutting some of his trees. When he contacted Bruce, Bruce said he would continue to do as he wanted. Eventually the issue went to court and the courts ruled in favor of the landowner.

In the 1920s a fire swept through the area. Eventually the lumber company shut down operations and the side tracks were pulled up. The Bruce name continued in the area until the 1940s.

INGER

1912 - 1955

CLASS C

APPROXIMATE LOCATION:
Near the junction of Itasca County Roads #35 and #146

For over 100 years, folks have been flocking to the area for fishing, hunting and the area's scenic and natural beauty. Long before the arrival of Europeans, the Inger area was an early Anishinabe settlement. The site was on a major water route. Later it was used as a logging waterway. The community of Inger (known as Shirt Tail City for unknown

Original Lakewood Lodge. (Courtesy of Lakewood Lodge, Inger, Minnesota)

Lakewood Lodge. (Courtesy of Lakewood Lodge, Inger, Minnesota)

reasons) was named for an early settler's Norwegian grandmother.

In 1910, early settler William Gibbs built the Riverside Hotel. The three-story building had twelve bedrooms on the second floor and was filled with fishermen and hunters visiting the area. The hotel was torn down, and the Inger Store was later built on the hotel site.

Inger did have its own school. For many years, the area's Native American children attending boarding schools far from home. By the 1930s the Native children began to attend school in Inger. According to lodge history, William and his wife, Mary had, at the time, three children. A teacher would come to Sand Lake only if there were seven or more children enrolled in school. William was able to get four Native children enrolled. The teacher boarded with a nearby family and taught school in their cabin. As enrollment increased, a small log cabin as built near the home. That became the first Inger School.

Early mail delivery was by backpack, later by horse. A post office was in operation from 1912 to 1954. Civilian Conservation Corps camps were in the area, including the Cut Foot Sioux camp.

Lakewood Lodge today. (Courtesy of Lakewood Lodge, Inger, Minnesota)

Resorts have been operating in the area for over one hundred years. In 1917, the Lakewood Lodge was built. At the time it was the largest cabin in Itasca County. It had a lobby, six sleeping rooms over the lobby, a dining room, kitchen, and two screened porches. All of the furniture was hand-made. Visitors from as far away as Chicago and the Twin Cities visited the lodge and often stayed for extended periods. They traveled by train to Deer River where William met them with horse and buggy for the two-day trip to the lodge. The lodge has had eight owners since 1906. In the 1950s, the original lodge was torn down and a new one built and used until 2006, when cabins and other remodeling was done.

Another historic lodge was the Williams Narrows Resort. The resort was established by Falver Williams, who had moved from Arizona to Minnesota due to respiratory problems in 1920. Originally consisting of four cabins, the resort now has all of the amenities one could ask for and is managed and owned by later generations of the Williams family.

Since those early days, Inger Township has reverted to being governmentally unorganized. Still a recreational destination, many flock to the region.

Jessie Lake Junction, 1909. (Author's collection)

JESSIE (JESSE) LAKE

1903 - 1954

CLASS A

APPROXIMATE LOCATION:
West of Marcell in Lake Jessie Township, Itasca County Roads #286 and #4 Northeast of Jesse Lake

Using alternate spellings, confusing, but no matter the spelling, Jessie Lake and Jesse Lake refer to the same location in Itasca County. Not only are there alternate spellings, the naming of the community has more than one version as well. The most common and accepted name came from a surveyor in the area during the 1870s and 1880s named Taylor. Taylor had a daughter, Jessie, for whom he named the nearby lake. The other version had the lake named for an early logger.

Built primarily for the area's logging operations, a station of the Minneapolis and Rainy River Railroad was built and named Jessie Lake in 1903. Upham tells that the junction had a general store and the only other buildings were for use by the railroad section crews. Not only did the loggers use the railroad, area residents used it for transportation, shipping and mail delivery. The early village included a small grocery store, a post office, telephone switchboard, depot, and section

house. A sawmill operated for a short while. Two churches were part of the community—Lutheran, the Norwegian Lutheran Church, and the Pilgrim (Swedish) Lutheran. The two churches later merged and are now known as the Jesse Lake Lutheran Church, located on the site of the original Pilgrim Church.

Midsummer Day (a Swedish Festival) and the Fourth of July were popular celebrations held annually. Baseball was also a popular activity.

The region had many one-room schoolhouses including the Jesse Lake School. Until 1931, it was a one-room school. Then a second room had to be added. The Minneapolis and Rainy River Railroad ceased to operate as did the grocery store in the late 1940s. The post office was discontinued in 1954. In later years, the community had several farms in the area including a tree farm and an ostrich farm.

LEIPOLD

1900 - 1910s

CLASS C

APPROXIMATE LOCATION:
Sago Township

Ten years after early settler Vincent Harrington arrived in Itasca County, others followed and settled in the region. So many settlers arrived that, in 1905, a school was needed. Built in 1905, at a cost of $770.00, the school was called the Harrington School. At that time, the Leipolds settled in the area. Since getting mail was difficult at best, especially in bad weather, John Leipold filed for a post office and became Leipold's first postmaster. Not coincidentally, the post office was also named for him.

Transportation was also difficult in the area and rail "speeders" were often used to travel. A speeder is a small rail car powered by a see-saw type handle system or paddles, sort of a "hand car" on rails. Social events were important to the community. In 1913, the Leipold Workingmans Society raised funds to buy one acre of land to be used for a town hall. Family get-togethers, Red Cross Drives, dances, and other events were popular. As transportation methods improved, Leipold declined, and in 1935 the rail tracks were pulled up.

SWAN RIVER

1890s – 1938 (to date)

CLASS A/D

APPROXIMATE LOCATION:
Junction of U.S. Highway #2 and Minnesota #65

Never an officially organized village, the small community of Swan River was known by four names, one for each of its four physical locations. Population waxed and waned as did the fortunes of the village.

The first location (1890 to 1891), now referred to as "Old Swan River" was established when the Duluth and Winnipeg Railroad constructed a rail line through the region. Thomas Feeley, founder of Feeley, later Warba, Minnesota) felt the best place for a town site was at the Continental Divide, where a strip of high land rose out of the mostly swampy landscape. Rumors were rampant that a north/south running railroad line would be constructed at the site. Feeley built a saloon and hotel. A store/post office and school were also part of the settlement. The Duluth and Winnipeg Railroad also had a small section house and telegraph office. When the Wright and Davis Railroad chose to locate their line a few miles to the east of Feeley's location, Feeley was astounded as he had thought that land unbuildable. Drainage efforts and ditching had dried the land enough to make it usable.

Soon a hotel, tavern, and restaurant, offering all you could eat for two bits, were established at the new location where the two rail lines intersected. Feeley had no choice but to abandon his location and move to the new site, known as Swan River Junction (1892 to 1899). The Junction location was busy and active. It also had a reputation as a rough and rowdy town.

Fights, stabbings and other commotions were common and frequent. The community did have its finer side and had a town orchestra, barbershop quartet, community ice skating rink and not so successful town baseball team. At one time a local photographer traveled the area taking photos of people and their homesteads, offering them for sale. Some of those photos still survive.

In 1898, a telephone line to Hibbing was completed. In 1899 the hotel burned. A new hotel that could accommodate 150 guests was built, but not at the Junction location, but in Swan River's third location known as East Swan River (1900 to 1940). Lasting forty years, the new location was less than one mile from Swan River Junction.

East Swan River experienced a growth spurt and within a short time a new railroad depot was built and the area's first forest ranger was stationed there. A fair was held in 1918, and in 1920 Standard Oil set up fuel tanks at the location. As logging activities declined, so did the railroad traffic and the community. A business revival in the 1920s and 1930s had several new businesses established including an auto repair garage. It is said the saloons were also doing a brisk business. As more businesses developed, they chose sites to the west of the community. The new area to the west became, logically West Swan River. In 1935 a tavern was built at the intersection of U.S. Highway #2 and Minnesota #65. Much of the area was destroyed by a tornado in 1938 and the village never fully revived.

The region and hamlet still carry the name Swan River and the post office is a rural branch.

TALMOON

1912 - 1954

CLASS A/G

APPROXIMATE LOCATION:
South of Highway #286 and Highway #6 Intersection

Claiming to be home to the "Minnesota's Oldest Bar" Hayslip's Corner was also the name of the community for a short time, from 1938 to 1939. Prior to that it was known as "Mack" from 1912 to 1938 and lastly as "Talmoon" from 1939 to 1954, at which time it became a rural branch post office. Talmoon is a variation of "Tal Moen" Swedish for "little hill in the pinewoods." That it is. The area was settled by Swedish immigrants. Today, the area is a mecca for recreational opportunities.

Talmoon Store and Post Office Postcard. (Author's Collection)

VERNA

1890 – 1910s

CLASS A/G

APPROXIMATE LOCATION:
¾ miles west of Warba, where Highway 10 crosses the railroad

When the Duluth and Winnipeg Railroad came to the region in 1899, they established a station referred to as Verna. Primarily a spur for the Verna Brick Company, a fast-growing settlement developed at the site.

Verna's first school, in 1898, was conducted in area homes. In 1901, School District #1 consisted of a school at Highway #2 and County Road #10. That lasted a short time until a larger school was built in 1903 at nearby Feeley. At the time, the old Verna School was moved and became a private home.

In 1894, Thomas Feeley built a sawmill less than one mile from Verna and the area became known as Feeley Spur. Many in the area felt that Feeley Spur was a good location for a town site, and, in 1904, the town of Feeley was established.

The two communities existed side-by-side for several years. In 1903 a general store was set up as well as a cook shack, bunk house, and a large barn to house the logging horses. A Baptist Church was built in 1904, but it was sold to the Lutherans in 1905. In 1905, a saloon and boarding house were constructed.

After a few years, Verna was on the decline and Feeley the growing community. In 1901 the post office was having trouble with mail getting mixed up between Foley and Feeley. Since Foley was the older of the towns, Feeley was told they had to rename their community. A contest was held and the name "Warba" (Ojibwe for resting place) was chosen and accepted. The Great Northern Railroad changed the depot's name from Verna to Warba and the two communities of Verna and Feeley merged to become Warba.

WAWINA

1912 - 1993

CLASS D

APPROXIMATE LOCATION:
East of Grand Rapids on U.S. Highway #2 and Itasca County Road #25

First inhabited by the area's Floodwood Indians, white settlement began in 1891 when a station of the Duluth and Winnipeg Railroad was established. Originally called Siding #6, it is not clear why or when the name Wawina (Ojibwe for "I remember him often") was adopted.

The community's first school was built near the train station in 1901. It burned in 1907 and was rebuilt on the same site. There was another school in the area, and that school offered English classes at night and helped prepare the area residents for the U.S. Citizenship test. The first religious services were held in 1908. A store and post office began in 1912. Produce and cattle shipments began in 1912. Soon the community included four general stores, a post office, confectionary, station/depot, and section house. An annual community fair was held and the 1919 featured attraction was a three-eared pig. The post office was discontinued in 1993. The region still carries the name "Wawina."

Kanabec County

Coin School being moved, Kanabec History Center. (Author's collection)

First Coin Store. (Courtesy of Kanabec History Center)

COIN

1899 - 1908

CLASS A

APPROXIMATE LOCATION:
Intersection of Kanabec County #4 and County #16

Coin, the town, may be gone, but folks can still shop at the "Coin School Christmas Shop." Unique hand-made items and just the right gift can be bought at the seasonal shop located in the historic Coin School on the grounds of the Kanabec History Center in Mora, Minnesota. The school was established in 1881 and closed in 1970. It was the last of Kanabec County's sixty-seven schools to close. In a major undertaking, the school was moved from Coin to the History Center in Mora. Visitors to the History Center can tour the historic school, view the historic photos, including photos of the move, and get a glimpse into the past. Each summer a pioneer Swedish school is conducted giving today's young students the experience of school in the early 1900s.

Coin also had a general store; the first burned and was replaced. A post office operated in the community from 1899 to 1908.

Coin School Shop. (Courtesy of the Kanabec History Center)

Second Coin store. (Courtesy of Kanabec History Center)

Coin School Interior. (Author's collection)

Coin School today. (Author's collection)

Koochiching County

Border school. (Courtesy of A. Filer)

Border school. (Courtesy of A. Filer)

BORDER

1912 - 1953

CLASS A

APPROXIMATE LOCATION:
MN #11 between UT139 and Town Road #140

At one time, Border had a station of the Canadian National Railroad. Border was also home to an early school, which still stands. Carved out of the wilderness, the area was prime logging country.

Bramble church. (Courtesy of T. Kremer)

Border school today. (Courtesy of A. Filer)

BRAMBLE

1928 - 1936

CLASS C

APPROXIMATE LOCATION:
Near intersection of MN #65 and Koochiching County #66

Perhaps the most enduring aspect of Bramble is the Russian Orthodox Church. The small community of Bramble was named for the prickly bush abundant in the region. The community spirit and passion for the church keeps it alive nearly one hundred years after its construction.

Bramble church today. (Courtesy of T. Kremer)

Built in 1918, the church was in disrepair in the 1930s and services were discontinued. In the 1960s descendants of Bramble's early settlers restored the church. Again in disrepair in the late twentieth century, residents rallied again to save the church. In 2010, according to a news article in *Hometown Focus*, the tiny church, only a few hundred square feet in area, played host to over forty people. Six singers from Russia provided authentic Russian music for the occasion. Donations were accepted and all funds raised were to be used in church restoration.

Bramble Orthodox church. (Courtesy of T. Kremer)

Craigville Hotel. (Courtesy of Judy Blais)

Craigville School. (Courtesy of Judy Blais)

The Grand Rapids Herald provided an update the following year. In August of 2011, it was reported that $14,500 dollars had been raised at the 2010 celebration. Crosses were restored, and the tower and dome were repainted using rubber based paint. The completion of the construction was also celebrated.

Today, Bramble is a long ago town but the Bramble Russian Orthodox Church and the community spirit live on. The church is on the National Register of Historic Places and preservation efforts continue.

CRAIGVILLE

1915 – 1952 (1970s)

CLASS A

APPROXIMATE LOCATION:
4 miles north of Effie along Koochiching County #5

At nearly every presentation I do, in almost every community I visit, someone asks about Craigville. It seems the small Koochiching County community has quite a reputation, and perhaps with good reason.

Craigville, first called Craig but changed to Craigville when it was learned another Craig existed, was just a railroad stop. Craigville was either the starting point or the end of the line for two railroads, the Minnesota, Dakota and Western and the Minneapolis, Rainy River, commonly known as the "Gut and Liver" line in part because of its frequent cargo of sausages. Things livened up when Camp 29 was established in 1913.

By 1915 Camp 29 had at least three hundred men working in the woods. Soon after a post office was established and a bootleg saloon was operating on the river. By the early 1920s a pool hall, and another bootleg joint or two were up and running. There was a constant turnover of "blind pigs," places illegally selling alcohol or selling illegal alcohol. Old timers ascertain that all of the liquor sold was illegal, no one had a license, maybe a federal stamp but no licenses. They also tell that it didn't take much to establish a saloon, just a couple of barrels with a board across for a bar. Since alcohol wasn't allowed in the logging camps, the lumberjacks had to head into Craigville to partake of the spirits. The jacks didn't worry about tomorrow, they worked for their Saturday night trips to town.

Craig logging camp. (Courtesy of Judy Blais)

In the mid 1970s, newspaper reporter Judy Blais wrote a series of articles on Craigville. Judy was familiar with the history of Craigville, had family in the area and interviewd several residents to capture the essence of Craigville in words, photos, and print. Previously unaware of the articles, I learned of them while at a presentation in Grand Rapids. Wally Glatz attended and very graciously gave me copies of the articles. The narratives, even thirty seven years later were fascinating, captivating and at times eye-opening. Recently Judy and I exchanged emails and letters, tales, history and the goal of preserving local history, in particular that of Craigville. With Judy's articles, input and permission, I share a few tales of Craig.

Craigville reached its heydey in the 1920s and 1930s, but lived long into the 1940s and a bit beyond. The community had a

The fishing trip. (Courtesy of Judy Blais)

population of 400-500, twenty-six saloons, one store, the post office, a lath mill and a depot. Main Street ran north/south from the bridge to the top of the hill. The street was lined with tar paper shacks and families lived east of Main Street in a section called Reid's Addition. Life-long resident, Pooch Liesenfeld told Judy that everyone figured the town wouldn't last more than six months so old boards and tar paper were used.

Pooch himself remembered one fishing trip in particular. Just a lad, he had heard of dynamiting fish. So he and another lad took six sticks of dynamite and some caps and went off down the railroad tracks to fish. They didn't get far when they met up with Pooch's dad and another man. Gingerly getting the explosives away from the boys, that was the end of those plans.

Contrary to most people's perception, the lumberjacks weren't bawdy and raucous all of the time. In fact, many tales tell that they were kind-hearted, generous and loved kids. They wouldn't hurt anyone. They would buy drinks for others until their money was gone, never thinking to hold onto it for themselves. They were also the first to take up a collection when someone needed help. That's not to say that rowdy behavior didn't take place. It did and often.

One time a fellow who was drunk fell over dead on top of the pool table. The guys playing pool dragged him off and put him under the table, continuing on with their game. He started to stink so they dragged him over to the depot where he stayed until the coroner arrived. Other drunks slept off the booze wherever they fell.

Another time some card sharks came to town with the intention of getting the jacks money. Folks didn't take kindly to someone cheating their jacks, so they asked the card sharks to leave. They didn't. So a couple of ropes were thrown over the beams and the card sharks were hung by their necks, with just their toes touching the floor. The next time they were asked to leave, they did.

Things were often violent. As one resident put it "Nobody even knows how many people were killed in Craigville." Judy tells of "burial at sea" or more precise, burial in the Big Fork River under the ice. The bodies wouldn't be discovered until spring thaw. Wanigans, floating cook shacks or in Craigville's case, floating saloons, were said to have trap doors where bodies could easily be disposed of. There wasn't much the law could do. Based in International Falls, it was a seventy-mile trip one way so law enforcement was nearly non-existent. Sure the law would stop by now and then, but "stop by" was about all they did.

The last log drives, usually an annual event, were in the early 1930s. With dwindling timber resources, the logging camps closed. The repeal of Prohibition signaled the end of Craigville. With no lumberjacks, the girls had nothing to do, so they left as well. The tar paper shacks eventually burned, and the area became a hunting region. In the 1940s there were three or four taverns left.

The stories go on and on, all in the same vein. Before leaving Craigville we should remember that Craigville was what it was. No judgements, no twenty-first-century morals—the times were what they were. People did the best they could with the circumstances they were given and Craigville was a product of the times, the circumstances and the people.

IN HER OWN WORDS
PEGGY MATTICE
CRAIGVILLE

In a place occupied by larger-than-life characters, she was perhaps the most colorful, the standout. With names such as Old Millie, Big Charlie, Tamarack Slim, Broken Ass Ole, Box Car Annie, Scarface Jean, and Dutch Mary, Peggy Mattice stood out. Known as Pretty Peggy, Peggy (Ann) Mattice was a formidable presence and the person I'm most asked about. Generally little is known about the men and women who lived lives in long-ago towns. Other than a few folk-lore tales and a blurb in a newspaper article or a book, if that, people lived their lives in relative obscurity, leaving little history behind and nothing of their thoughts or memories. However, in the case of Peggy, we have a hidden treasure of her story, in her own words.

In 1972, a *Minneapolis Star Tribune* columnist interviewed Peggy. Judy Blais, a news reporter for *The International Falls Journal* did a series of articles in 1977 on Craigville, including an interview with Peggy. Most revealing and unique is an interview on file with the Minnesota Historical Society. In the mid-1970s, as part of the Forest History Oral History Project, audio recordings were made of interviews with many participants in the early logging camps and northern communities. The recordings as well as written transcripts preserve the history of the times and the places, in the participants' own words. So not only do we have the verbatim transcripts, but we can hear their stories and tales in their own words. We can learn about Peggy's past, her thoughts, her memories and can hear her actual voice. It is a true treasure. Using those interviews it is possible to learn more about Peggy.

Peggy was born in Eveleth Minnesota in 1903. When she was a child the family moved to Bovey where Peggy's father had a store. A move to Virginia followed, and Peggy went to Roosevelt High School. After high school she studied nursing at St. Mary's Hospital in Duluth. Peggy later moved to the Twin Cities where she worked at the Emporium, an upscale department store. In the 1930s she lived in a plush apartment in the Summit Hill neighborhood of St. Paul.

Her guests were from some of the best families and some were well-known political figures of the time. The 1930s were the heydeys of gangster and Prohibition. Peggy knew many of them, including Baby Face Nelson, Doc Barker, Alvin Karpis, John Dillinger, and "all those guys." She recalled that they were all good looking and were just like other people. They didn't act tough, although she said it was embarrassing to be dancing with a man whose coat kept pulling up and exposing the gun on his hips. Some wanted Peggy to travel with them but she was too smart to be a gangster's moll and always advised others against it. One woman didn't heed the warnings and her body, as well as that of her gangster boyfriend, were found in a farm field shot to death.

Peggy confessed that she was married, once, in 1940. There is no mention of who or what happened. Her life changed in 1940. Her mother died and with severe recurring asthma attacks that seemed better when she was in the north woods she decided to find a place as far back in the woods as possible. Someone referred her to Craigville. She had never seen a lumberjack before and had heard they were rough, rowdy and crude. However, she found them, at times, meek, generous and good.

When arriving in Craigville, she became a partner in a tavern. The eighty-year-old proprietor offered her half interest if she would stay and run the tavern, telling her the jacks would rather look at her than him. Peggy stayed and within a few years bought out the tavern and made it her own. Making improvements that none of the other taverns had, Peggy proudly said, "I'm the only place that had running water, baths, a toilet." She also put tile on the floor, installed plumbing, added new siding and a new roof, and "fixed it all up." Previously her building had been the former grocery store.

Peggy recalled that when someone got drunk and fell on the floor, that's where they stayed. She'd never seen anything like it. "I thought they should be helped up." Generally amiable to answering any and all questions in the interviews, at times she seemed hesitant, reluctant, and evasive. In one interview she is asked point blank if she was the "madame." "Not really." She went on to explain that she did have girls, of course "all of the places did. We had to, but I never took a cut from any of them. The money they made was their own." She added that it was a profession like anything else. She never encouraged anyone herself as she didn't think it a very healthly occupation.

Peggy did step in every now and then when she encountered people in difficulties. She tells of a married man with half a dozen kids who didn't have enough to eat. Out of the corner of her eye she saw him going down the hall with one of the girls.

She grabbed him by the scruff of the neck and told him he was going the wrong way. The girl got mad as well, but Peggy couldn't help that. A guy with a wife and kids without enough to eat didn't need to be spending his money like that. She again reiterated she did not make money off the girls; they simply "stimulated business." The last call girl was reported to leave in 1950.

There were no churches in Craigville, just an old lean-to that sometimes hosted services. Since Peggy was Catholic, she said she went to Effie or Bigfork for mass. As she summed up her years, "I never killed anybody or anything so I guess I can't be that bad."

Peggy ran the tavern for over thirty years. In 1972 she was mostly retired. She didn't open up much in winter but in summer was open. She built a new house, painted blue, on the hill. In 1977 only a few shacks remained, but, oh, the stories and tales, and the characters—they live on still. Hearing Peggy's own words is like experiencing the history of the area on a personal face-to-face basis. Peggy was indeed a colorful character as well. Hear her story at the Minnesota Historical Societies collections page.

FAIRLAND

1902 - 1936

CLASS A

APPROXIMATE LOCATION:
42 Miles from International Falls, On County #101 (Black River Road)

Soon after the area was opened up to homesteaders in the early 1900s, three bachelors made their claims. The land was rich virgin timber near the headwaters of the Black River. The settlement was first known as Feldman until 1912, but the name was later changed to Fairland after the

Long ago Fairland building. (Courtesy of A. Filer)

Fairland School marker. (Courtesy of A. Filer)

Early Fairland Store and Post Office. (Author's collection)

Fairland Store and Post Office marker. (Courtesy of A. Filer)

Fairland today. (Courtesy of A. Filer)

early settler's home place. A general store and a school were established in 1912. First classes were held in an abandoned cabin.

Some came to the region only to harvest the timber and then left. The community also had a small library. Several community organizations were active and included a Jolly Homemakers Club.

The high cost of maintaining the roads and other improvements in the isolated area resulted in the New Deal's Resettlement program relocating the settlers.

HAPPYLAND

1908 - 1935

CLASS A

APPROXIMATE LOCATION:
3 Miles East of US. #71 and County #77

With a name like Happyland, there must be a story behind the name. Supposedly, there are several versions on the origin of the name. The one that is most often repeated is that, in the early logging days, crews would get their Saturday pay and head to the nearest town to spend it. The spongy muskeg made it difficult walking. When the hikers came to higher ground, a few miles from the settlement, the walking vastly improved, thus making happy hikers, and Happyland.

First settled about 1904, Happyland also included a depot and flag stop. The outgoing mail bag was placed on a crane, and when the railroad passed through it grabbed it on the fly. Incoming mail would be delivered the same way. Sometimes it would be tossed out a ways from the depot and would be lost in the snow until spring.

A Koochiching County history book writes that one resident on his way back to Happyland from the Minneapolis/St. Paul area in 1914 asked for a ticket to Happyland. The busy clerk, with long lines of impatient travelers, was not amused by the joke. Insisting it wasn't a joke, the resident pressured the harried clerk finally to look it up. The clerk found there actually was a Happyland, and issued the ticket.

The community post office was established in 1909 and was discontinued in 1935.

PELLAND

1902 - 1918

CLASS A

APPROXIMATE LOCATION:
Near intersection of U.S. #71 and MN #11 on the Rainy River

When Quebec natives Frank and Joe Pelland, with their families, arrived in the area in 1894, the region was wilderness. They settled near the confluence of the Rainy and Little Fork rivers.

In 1901 a post office was established. A general store began operating that same year. The area's large Native American population often brought venison, fish, and other items into the store. The first school classes were in a cabin. Little else is known.

WAYLAND

1911 - 1935

CLASS A

APPROXIMATE LOCATION:
Beltrami Island State Forest, Indian Pines Road approximately five miles east of Highway #72

Wayland's first mail came by launch and was delivered by foot. The carrier only delivered first class mail, as newspapers, catalogs and other items made the load too heavy. The community had a post office and a school. When it became apparent the railroad would not come to the region, and as the timber was logged off, many of the settlers left the region. It is now part of the Beltrami Island State Forest.

Pelland today. (Courtesy of A. Filer)

Wayland 2014. (Courtesy of A. Filer)

Wayland School. (Courtesy of A. Filer)

Wayland today. (Courtesy of A. Filer)

Lake County

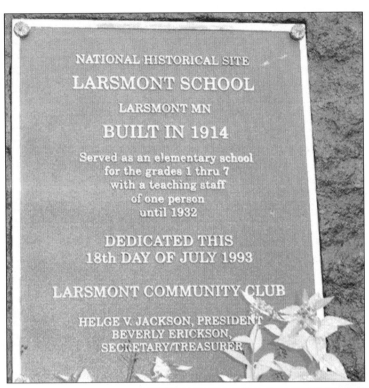

Larsmont marker. (Author's collection)

Larsmont School. (Author's collection)

LARSMONT

1915 - 1978

CLASS C

APPROXIMATE LOCATION:
6 miles south of Two Harbors on Scenic Highway #61

The little red schoolhouse celebrated its 100th birthday in 2014. A large community celebration was held with two full days of activities in honor of the charming landmark. It was even possible to travel to the event by railroad from Duluth. The North Shore Scenic Railroad offered special fares and pre-arranged stops and pickups. Local news media covered the event. and for that time Larsmont was bustling and thriving.

Originally called Milepost 22 because of its location along the Duluth, Missabe and Iron Range Railroad, the community's name was changed when the post office was established. The Finnish settlers had wanted to name it after the home place in Finland, Larsmo. However the postal service suggested a more "American" name be used. So "nt" was added, in reference to the region's many hills.

Most records agree that the first settlers to the region, in 1889, were the three Thompson brothers from Norway. They had originally tried farming and later turned to commercial fishing. The Duluth, Missabe and Iron Range Railroad had recently been completed from Duluth to Two Harbors, running through the Larsmont area. In 1913 an old wagon trail was graveled and became the Old North Shore Road. In 1922 the new Highway #61 was built above the tracks. It was paved in 1928. The expressway was opened in the early 1960s.

Logging pulpwood was the area's first industry, fishing was soon to follow. With Lake Superior so close by and with skilled craftsmen in the region it was only natural that boat building blossomed. A fleet of freighters, sixty-five feet long and known as the "Mosquito Fleet" was built in Larsmont. One of the best known builders, Charles Hill and John Coson built the *Crusader I* and the *Crusader II*. Crown Prince Olav of Norway christened the *Crusader II* with a bottle of Lake Superior water. After years of service, the ship is now on display in Two Harbors near the lakefront and the Two Harbors Lighthouse Bed and Breakfast. An Isle Royale excursion boat, sailboats, fishing boats and skiffs were also built in Larsmont.

A post office was first established in 1915. Prior to that the mail had been delivered by the legendary John Beargrease. From 1915 until the 1950s mail was delivered to the region by train and after 1950 by mail truck from Duluth. Local news reports relate that in 1978, the postmaster asked for a $150.00 a month raise. His salary of $191.00 per month had not been

Larsmont School outhouse. (Author's collection)

Larsmont School sign. (Author's collection)

Larsmont School today. (Author's collection)

increased in over twelve years. The postal service offered an $8.00 a month increase. The post master declined. The six-day-a-week, eight-hour-a-day job was then offered to other area residents, but there were no takers. Thus the post office was discontinued and mail came from Two Harbors.

The tourist cabin business began in the 1920s and reached its peak in the mid-1930s when the area was home to over 100 cabins. Today, tourist cabins still attract many to the Larsmont area.

Chicken farms, raising turkeys and silver fox and mink farms were also active.

Symbolizing the community the Larsmont School was built in 1914. The first school bus was an old wagon box mounted on an old Republic truck. It transported high school students to Two Harbors. When a snow plow was needed, two buses worked in tandem with a plow in front. The school closed in 1932 and was sold to the community in 1934 for $200.00.

Countless events were and are still held at the building. The first church services were held in the school. Most social activities centered on the church including Fourth of July celebrations, a Thanksgiving dinner, and an Annual Picnic. Once autos became the mode of transportation, folks traveled to Two Harbors for church services. It is also available for special events. The school is on the National Register of Historic Places and countless travelers stop for a respite at the school grounds while traveling the scenic North Shore Drive.

Community involvement is and always has been or cornerstone of Larsmont. A cornucopia of community groups were active in Larsmont and many still are. Among them were the Ladies Aid, a Farmer's Club, 4-H, Community Club, a Larsmont-Knife River Conservation Club and a volunteer fire department and Ladies Auxillary.

The settlement was built on community spirit and it thrives today on that spirit. Larsmont as a town may no longer exist but the charming red schoolhouse and the warm hearts of area residents keep Larsmont and its heritage and history alive.

Lake of the Woods County

Carp community center. (Courtesy of T. Kremer)

Carp. (Courtesy of T. Kremer)

Carp from the south. (Courtesy of T. Kremer)

Carp from the north. (Courtesy of T. Kremer)

CARP

1912 - 1933

CLASS C

APPROXIMATE LOCATION:
Lake of the Woods County #1 midway between County's
#16/84 and County #86

Early settlers liked the name "Carp." It was short, it was different, and it was specific. So the community that began as Knutson became Carp. The name supposedly reflected the plentiful carp in the area's rivers but what at first so many thought were carp really weren't. The fish people saw in abundance were actually Buffalo Red Suckers.

A Lake of the Woods County history book tells that the best timber in the Rainy River area was in the Carp area. Forty acres out of every 160 homestead claim had river frontage. It didn't take long before all the lands were claimed.

Timber was, without a doubt, the lure of the area. Many came to the region with no intention of staying long, just long enough to harvest the timber. Logging companies arrived about 1910, chief among them was the Rainy River Timber Company. They set up a logging camp just one-half mile west of Carp. Annual timber drives occurred each spring. One hundred men worked around the clock to keep the logs flowing downstream. The last log drive was in 1929.

Carp served as a jumping off point for those heading or homesteading to points south. A post office was established in 1909 and was discontinued in the early 1930s. Hansen's Store operated from 1915 until 1958 and was open 365 days a year.

The first school term was held in 1910 and ran for three months. The first classes were held at the timber company's camp. In 1912 a school building was constructed and operated until a new, fully modern school was built in 1921. There were approximately seventy students. In 1969 the school consolidated with the Baudette School system.

In 1921 the Carp Hall was built with volunteer labor. The native tamarack log building was twenty-four by thirty-six feet and it hosted many area social events including dances, club meetings, Fourth of July celebrations and also served as the local polling place. A new larger building was constructed in 1935/1936 and is still actively used.

The community had two churches, a short-lived Catholic Church and a Baptist Church housed in a former Lutheran church moved to Carp from Hackett in 1954.

Carp plaque. (Courtesy of T. Kremer)

As timber resources declined the land was repurposed for agricultural use. During the Depression some area farmers were very prosperous. According to a Lake of the Woods history book, one farmer bought a new Chevrolet, went to the World's Fair and came home with $200.00 in his pocket. Those times were not to last.

During World War II, new settlers arrived but the good land had long been claimed. Some attempted farming the marginal lands but with little success. To supplement their meager incomes many turned to trapping. With weasel pelts garnering .75 to $1.25 each and each mink pelt earning $2.00 to $3.00, it was good money. Wages at the time were only $1.00 per day.

Many community organizations were active throughout Carp's life. Some such as the Home Club are still going strong. Others included, the Farmers Club, the Yeoman Lodge, Peppsters Club and the Carp Baseball team (Rapid River Carp Club, 1938 to 1948).

A historical marker was placed in Carp and pays tribute to the early pioneers and testifies to Carp's history and legacy.

CLEMENTSON

1901 - 1964

CLASS C

APPROXIMATE LOCATION:
11 miles east of Baudette on Minnesota #11

Starting with a small trading post in 1901 and eventually expanding to a well-stocked general store, Clementson was soon the main supply center for the logging operations in

Eidem School. (Courtesy of Linda Lafkey)

Silver Creek Church. (Courtesy of Linda Lafkey)

Clementson Rapids postcard. (Author's collection)

the area. Before long a second store was added. Merchandise for the stores was brought in by launch and railroad. The store was destroyed by fire in the 1950s.

The Clementsons arrived in 1896 and were the first settlers in the area. The area was high ground with vast timber supplies and scenic beauty. The nearby rapids and waterfall where the Rapid River and Rainy River meet was a popular site. In the early days a steamboat was popular.

After the first trading post other businesses joined the community. By 1908 a hotel, saloon, sawmill, and shingle mill had become part of the village. In 1913 a telephone line connected

Clementson to Spooner via Warroad. Later that year a road connected the two communities as well.

As the timber resources dwindled, the logging mills were closed and moved to new locations. Clementson's importance as a trade center diminished as well.

During World War II, Oscar Clementson built eight cabins along the Rainy River and operated a summer resort. Another, Robert's Resort with four cabins operated until the 1960s.

The area schools consolidated with Baudette in the 1990s. The post office, established in 1901 became a rural station in 1964 and was discontinued in the 1990s. Linda Lafkey, whose

Clementson Rapids today. (Courtesy of A. Filer)

Clementson today. (Courtesy of A. Filer)

family were original settlers and longtime residents recalled how important the schools and churches were to the area residents. Many social activities were centered around both. One school, named for her family was an active place and remains on family land.

Clementson is still a scenic site and resorts in the area still invite you to visit the Clementson area.

GRACETON

1905 - 1973/DATE

CLASS D

APPROXIMATE LOCATION:
West of Baudette on MN #11 at junction of County #4

Since steam engines need water every few miles, a water tower was built, a town site platted and a store was established in the hopes that a thriving community would develop. The new town site was given a name, Graceton, after the conductor's newborn daughter, Grace. The only problem, no water was available for the train engines. Thus the water tower and the site were abandoned.

Just a quarter mile east of the abandoned site, the Canadian National Railroad had previously constructed a section house.

A store and saloon had been established next to the section house. The store owner petitioned for the post office to be moved 3,000 feet from its earlier location to his store site. When approved, the new town site location became known as East Graceton. According to a Lake of the Woods County History book, in a segment written by Terry Tofte, things took off from there.

Most of the settlers were young single men although there were plenty of single women. Several were widows with young children to support and many took in washing and mending to make a living. Most settlers had a root cellar which they filled with potatoes, carrots, and rutabagas. Canned goods lined the shelves. Blueberries and other berries were put up in jams, which tasted darn good on the hand-churned ice cream at the annual Fourth of July celebrations.

Cedar forests were abundant, and demand for wood was high. Cedar yards sprang up on the south side of the railroad tracks. In 1905, land was donated for a school. The first term was six months long. By 1910 Graceton had one hundred residents, a saloon, a blacksmith, restaurant, and a house of ill repute.

There were at least two churches, the Graceton Congregational Church of Cedar Spur and the Swedish Lutheran Church of Graceton. Due to declining membership the Swedish Lutheran Church closed in 1922. The building was moved to Roosevelt and became the Mt. Carmel Church.

Graceton today. (Courtesy of A. Filer)

In October of 1910, a raging forest fire swept through the region. No lives were lost in the Graceton area but many buildings were destroyed. Rebuilding began almost immediately. Soon four stores, a café, a post office, and at least seven saloons were up and running. A cedar yard and feed store were also established. The feed store later became the dance hall and was known as Austin Long's Fireside Inn. It burned in 1941 and was not rebuilt.

The Lake of the Woods Telephone Company began in 1913 and operated until 1962 when it was bought out by the People's Coop Telephone Company. A post office was established in 1905, closed in 1910 and reopened in 1913. It operated until 1973 when Graceton became a rural station. The Farmer's State Bank of Graceton began operating in 1917. Due to lack of business, it merged with the First State Bank of Williams in 1926. The Graceton bank building was later moved to Williams where it housed the Williams Post Office.

After the 1910 fire a new schoolhouse was built, and in 1912 fifty students attended. By 1931 the school was too small, so a lean-to was added as was another teacher. Terry Tofte's history tells that at one point in the school's history, a scandal had everyone abuzz with gossip. Unable to find a teacher, a married woman filled the position. The town was appalled. Sure women taught school, but not married women. In those days (even up until the 1960s), once a female teacher got married her teaching days were over. Why, having a married woman teach school was downright indecent. When school resumed after the Christmas break, it was obvious the teacher was pregnant. Enough was enough. She simply could not be allowed to teach young children in that condition. She was abruptly relieved of her duties and a male was recruited to take over the reins of the classroom.

The Yeoman's Hall was a social gathering place and meeting hall. During World War I women met there to knit clothes for America's Expeditionary Forces in Europe. The community also had a baseball team complete with monogrammed wool uniforms. Even though travel was difficult, the team travelled as far away as Thief River Falls and International Falls for games.

As the timber resources dwindled many left the area; others turned to farming. By 1930 declining enrollment left Graceton without a school. The lack of jobs forced people to leave the area and businesses closed or were abandoned. World War II called many local men and several women left to do war-related work. Most of the young people that left never returned to the area. Graceton's boom years were over, and the town was on the decline. By 1992, it was primarily a rural community with a few businesses and a highway sign to mark the town.

HACKETT

1905 - 1923

CLASS C

APPROXIMATE LOCATION:
2 miles south of Wheeler Point at the intersection of MN #172 and County #32

The first business was a trading post started by early settler John Hackett. Soon there were several stores in the area including Loughan's in 1907 and Mrs. Ole Johnson's. Mrs. Johnson's store was located at what was known as Brevick's Corner at the intersection of Minnesota Highway #172 and County Highway #32. It operated until the late 1940s.

Mink ranching was flourishing in the area in the 1930s to the 1960s. A coop fishing venture provided rough fish to the mink farmers as mink feed, and the walleyes were shipped to Chicago and New York. In 1942 a large freezer plant was built to store mink feed, but it never worked properly. So the plant was converted to living quarters. The building was later made into a potato warehouse. Demand decreased and prices declined, and, with the introduction of "fake" fur, the end of mink farmer was inevitable. The last mink farm closed in 1969.

The early Hackett School was replaced with a modern two-room building constructed by the WPA in 1936. Known as the Wheeler School it closed in 1971. The building was sold and was maintained by an area family.

Hackett today. (Courtesy of A. Filer)

LOVEDALE

1919 - 1935

CLASS A

APPROXIMATE LOCATION:
20 Miles south of Pitt on the south branch of the Rapid River

Settlers in the region spread out along the branch of the Rapid River. A dance hall was built and hosted many dances and other social gatherings. The first school term was in 1914 and fourteen students attended. After three years the school consolidated and students went to Rako or Bankton schools. A post office operated from 1919 until 1935. Little else is known about the community.

PEPPERMINT CREEK

1904 - 1940s

CLASS A

APPROXIMATE LOCATION:
6 Miles south of Pitt on County Roads #6/3/173, Walhalla Township

Settled in 1904 little is known about the small community. A Lake of the Woods history book notes that the Peppermint Creek school was the center of the community. The building was located in three different spots. It also served as a meeting place, hosted church services and other community events. The school closed in the 1940s.

PITT

1903 - 1993

CLASS C

APPROXIMATE LOCATION:
Near intersections of MN #11, County Roads #6/212 and County #167 (Pitt Road NW)

Based on a railroad/timber economy, the Pitt area was kept busy by both. It also had something every railroad needed, ballast—crushed stone and rocks used as a track bed. Ballast is packed below, between and around rail ties. It facilitates drainage, keeps down vegetation that might otherwise interfere with track stability and supports significant loads. Pitt had a deposit of rich gravel, perfect for ballast. The gravel was loaded by steam shovel in to railroad cars. The "pit" of gravel gave "Pitt" its name.

A post office was established as was the first store in 1903. The store was two miles west of the station. In 1906 a sawmill operated and a Canadian National depot was operating. Due to the heavy shipping schedules, the depot was staffed twenty-four hours a day. Soon two blacksmiths, three cedar yards and a school were part of the Pitt community. A massive forest fire swept through the region in 1910, destroying many buildings, and many communities. Pitt was heavily damaged, but it did recover. As the timber industry gave way to agriculture, Pitt was able to make that adjustment too.

A road connecting Pitt to Graceton, called the Elwell Road, was completed in 1914. Most of the businesses in Pitt were located on the south side of the tracks, and the town site was platted on the north side. Many businesses planned to move

Pitt 2014. (Courtesy of A. Filer)

Pitt today. (Courtesy of A. Filer)

to the town. A hotel with a pool hall was built. The Elkins Store became the Pitt Mercantile, and Pitt was booming and became the trade center for the region, including Lovedale.

A Yeoman's Lodge was built in 1914 and had over one hundred members. A church was organized in 1920 with services provided by various ministers. Both a Farmer's Club and a Farm Bureau were established in the early 1920s. A potato warehouse was constructed.

Due to dwindling timber supplies, the Canadian National Railroad petitioned to close the depot. After extended legal and court proceedings, the depot was closed in the 1930s. The Pitt School consolidated with Baudette Schools in 1968. In 1991, the store was closed and the post office was discontinued.

Today a 4-H Park, a community church, homes, and storage buildings are in the Pitt area. A highway sign points the directions and the "Pitt News" is still covered in *The Baudette Region*.

RAKO

1919 - 1936

CLASS A

APPROXIMATE LOCATION:
Keil Township, SE Lake of the Woods County within boundaries of Beltrami Island State Forest, SW of County #77

Electricity took a long time acoming to the Rako area. In fact, the region was the very last place in all of Minnesota to get electrical service. Because of the small number of area residents and the high costs of installing power services, intense lobbying efforts by residents and county commissioners were required to get the services installed.

Rako was the most southerly settlement in Lake of the Woods County and was named for County Board member A.E. Rako. Settlement began after 1905 and peaked by 1920, when nearly every 160-acre homestead in the county was claimed. The heaviest influx of settlement was after 1912. In those early days, it was believed drainage and ditching efforts would result in farmable land. Rumors had two railroads coming to the region. But the railroads didn't come, and the dredging and ditching efforts were a failure, though the channels created were later used as road beds. Access to the region was limited to the ditched grades but they too were nearly impassable. Bog trails and creek sides did allow some travel. As a result, Rako was little more than a post office and school settlement.

A post office operated from 1919 until 1936. The first three school terms were held in early settler's homes. In 1918 student enrollment was such that two new schools were built in the area. In 1935, a new school was built by the WPA (Works Progress Administration). The WPA also constructed an airport, more like a grass landing strip. Named the Keil Airport after the township, it was hoped air access would aid in connecting the remote settlement. It was abandoned upon completion. As late as the 1990s the strip could be seen from the air.

The population of the region was hit hard during the 1940s but a small core of families kept the community alive for another forty years. According to a Lake of the Woods history book, as older residents died or left not enough residents came into Rako to be called a community. Most lands are now used for hunting and other seasonal recreational pursuits. The area is now part of the Beltrami Island State Forest and the Rako town site is marked on the forest maps.

Marshall County

Ellerth cemetery. (Courtesy of A. Filer)

Ellerth today. (Courtesy of A. Filer)

Englund store front. (Courtesy of A. Filer)

Englund 2014. (Courtesy of A. Filer)

BIG WOODS

1886 - 1909

CLASS A

APPROXIMATE LOCATION:
Near Intersection of Marshall County #139 and #220

As the small group of covered wagons made their way from Willmar to the Snake River in 1878, the travelers decided the site was the logical place for a settlement. It was far enough away from the towns of Argyle and Stephen to be practical, and the region offered the farming opportunities they were looking for. They immediately began to clear land and make homes. Months after arriving, a prairie fire swept through the area destroying everything including food for the livestock. The settlers had to scour the countryside in search of unburned swamp land to be used as feed. A few years later, in 1882, floods ravaged the region. Cattle had to be moved to higher ground. Still the floods swept away 700 fence posts, 1,400 fence rails and logs. Mosquitos were a never-ending nuisance. Still the settlers persevered.

A ferry was built across the Red River in 1891. A loading elevator that transferred grain to a 1,000-bushel-capacity barge was kept so busy a line of ten barges were towed by steamboat and were lined up waiting to be loaded. Several steamboats, including the government boat *Ogema* provided transportation from Big Woods to Grand Forks, a trip of twelve hours each way.

Big Woods businesses included a sawmill, a couple of stores (one with a post office that operated from 1886 until 1909), and two churches. The town was the social center of the region. Many events were held at the Woodsmen Hall and a town brass band provided entertainment.

ELLERTH

1898 - 1913

CLASS A

APPROXIMATE LOCATION:
Intersection of Marshall County #4 and #28

Before becoming the Marsh Grove Store, it was known as the Ellerth and Korstad Store. Built in 1890, the store included a post office. The town's name came from the fact that the first store and post office were in the Ellerth Sagness home. The community also had the Fairview School, the Bethesda Church, and a telephone exchange. After 1929 the store building was used for storage and living quarters. Nothing else is known about the community. A cemetery and town hall building are still at the intersection.

ENGLUND

1899 - 1908

CLASS C

APPROXIMATE LOCATION:
6 miles west of Minnesota #59 on Marshall County #5

In the mid-1880s the closest town to Englund was Stephen. People had to walk or take their oxen to town for supplies and the mail. When one family went to town, they would often bring back their neighbors' mail and supplies. Finally a store was built and a post office established. The post office operated from 1899 to 1908. The community's school lasted sixty-six years, from 1903 to 1969. Englund's school was the last ungraded school in Marshall County. The store building is still standing, though the sign spells Englund incorrectly.

Englund Pepsi. (Courtesy of A. Filer)

Englund today. (Courtesy of A. Filer)

FLORIAN

1903 - 1908

CLASS C

APPROXIMATE LOCATION:
Near intersection of Marshall County Roads #1 and #6

Stanislog Gryglazewski is quite a mouthful to pronounce, even for the Polish immigrants who had settled in the area. Florian Matuszewski was much easier so the town's original name of Stanislawlo was changed to Father Florian Matuszewski's first name. Nearby Grygla was named in honor of Gryglazewski.

In the early years a stage coach line ran from Stephen to Greenbush, dropping mail at Englund. Florian area resident Peter Kwjawa walked to Englund and brought mail back to Florian. From 1900 to 1909 mail was by mail carrier from Strandquist.

The small community consisted of a grocery store with a gas pump in later years. The pump is said to be the only remaining remnant. The parish of the Assumption Church was also part of the community. A Florian Society Hall and the Polish National Alliance Lodge hosted many a wedding as well as other events and celebrations.

Assumption Church, Florian. (Courtesy of A. Filer)

Florian today. (Courtesy of A. Filer)

GATZKE

1901 - 2010

CLASS D

APPROXIMATE LOCATION:
East of Middle River and NW of Grygla on County Road #6
near intersection of Minnesota Highway #89

One of the more recent post office closures, Gatzke's post office operated for over one hundred years from 1901 until 2010. Though not a required component of a town or community, a post office provided a solid identity. Many times a community outlived its post office, yet it was during the post office years the town and community was established and was at its peak years. Sill a community's life-span is not always dictated by a post office. Gatzke population and businesses may have declined, but Gatzke still has a physical presence. Whereas many lost towns are long ago towns, Gatzke's physicality is still evident in the region. Unlike many long ago communities, most area residents remember and recall Gatzke as a town, and the site is still Gatzke to most.

Settlers first came to the area in 1897. The first post office was one and one-half miles from the present town site. It was named after the first postmaster's wife—Gatzke was her maiden name. In 1905, a store was built near the post office. Mail was hauled to the Gatzke post office by a horse and two-wheeled cart from Breese, near Middle River.

A creamery was built in 1907 and soon a blacksmith, shoe repair, town hall, hardware, and bank joined the community as well. With changing transportation and altering lifestyles, Gatzke slowly declined and is today a rural hamlet.

Gatzke Cafe. (Courtesy of A. Filer)

Gatzke today. (Courtesy of A. Filer)

Gatzke post office, 2010. (Courtesy of J. Gallagher/Post Mark Collectors Club)

RADIUM

1905 - 1984

CLASS A

APPROXIMATE LOCATION:
Approximately 5 miles northeast of Warren on Marshall County #35

The Radium post office was discontinued, just thirty years ago in 1985. Slowly declining through the late twentieth century, Radium was at its peak in the early 1900s. The Marshall County community was named for the newly discovered metallic element of the same name.

The Soo Line Railroad came through the region in 1905. The first block of the new town site was sold to the school. Soon a one-room school was built and filled to capacity. Most students did not speak English, and many had to walk over three miles to get to school. In the early years, the school term was three months in the spring and three months in the fall. The state paid a small sum for students who attended school forty days a year. Some parents misunderstood, thinking their children only had to attend forty days total. So once their children hit that forty day benchmark, they kept them home to help out around the home and farms. In 1914, with over sixty students, another room was added as well as a library and cloakroom. Later a well was drilled and was used by area residents as much as by the school, as many homesteads did not have their own water wells.

Since many students had to walk more than three miles to get to school, several hitched their homemade wooden toboggans to the family horse and were pulled to school. One school board member thought teachers needed more to do so providing hot lunches for the students was added to their list of duties. For a while the older girls made lunches but the most popular and most convenient way to provide hot lunches was the "pint jar" method. Students brought food from home in a glass pint jar. Once arriving at school, the jars would be put in a pan of cold water, near the stove. By noon, hot lunches were ready to eat. The school consolidated with the Warren Schools and in 1963 the school building was sold and moved. The land was also sold and was highly prized because of the water well.

The community of Radium was bustling and busy. The community included a hotel that burned in 1910 (a man was charged and convicted of starting the fire with a candle), the hardware store with a light-generating plant in the basement (which provided electricity for the town and also had upstairs apartments), a blacksmith, another hotel with a confectionary store, a restaurant and dance hall, and a bank from 1910 until 1925. A lumberyard, post office, and a saloon and restaurant were also part of the community. The saloon/restaurant were later sold to the Woodsmen and even later used as a Community Hall until a new one was constructed in the 1950s. A barber was set up in the saloon, but since he didn't have a license he could not charge for his services. Most donated twenty-five cents for his services. A cream station was in operation from 1907/1908 and later became a cheese factory. That closed when they couldn't get

Radium Siding today. (Courtesy of A. Filer)

Radium today. (Courtesy of A. Filer)

enough milk. Later the building was destroyed by fire. A Soo Line Depot was built in 1907. The two-story building had a waiting room, ticket office, and storage space on the first floor. Depot agents lived on the second floor.

Radium had three elevators all operating during the same time period. The Spaulding Elevator was later moved to Thief River Falls. The Atlantic Elevator was the smallest and was later moved to another location by rail. The Northern Elevator was later moved by rail to North Dakota.

Radium is still marked by a highway sign and the area has a rural population.

ROSEWOOD

1912 - 1954

CLASS C

APPROXIMATE LOCATION:
Northwest of Thief River Falls on County #11, just west of MN #59

Fourth of July celebrations were special in Rosewood. People looked forward to the festivities all year long. Favorite memories include the shooting gallery stand, the tug-of-war between the city folks and the farmers, and the booth where a man stuck his head through a sheet and let people throw eggs at him. Baseball was the highlight of the day and drew big crowds. People from near and far came, some even riding the train from Thief River Falls. Speakers, music, and firecrackers filled the air and brought the festivities to an end.

Medicine shows were also special events. The barkers thought up all sorts of gimmicks to get folks in the buying mood for the alcohol laden "blood purifiers" they sold. One included having a bare foot man jump into a tub of glass shards. The elixirs they sold could cure everything or so they said. At the least the alcohol made people feel like they could do anything. Traveling horse and buggy salesmen frequented the area and sold Watkins and Raleigh products.

Every now and then a circus came to town. A tent was erected near the railroad tracks and area residents, young and old, flocked to see the shows and attractions. Trained dogs, mules, acrobats, and an elephant were common side shows. One time, an elephant with a new trainer, bolted, knocking down a tent stake and collapsing the tent. The elephant dented a new Chevy and took the headlight out. Panic set in and people rushed to safety on the railroad loading dock. The elephant was found the next day, two miles from town, standing in a swamp.

Settled by Norwegians, Rosewood was set on a high ridge that ran north and south. Called Trysil Ryggen by the Norwegians, Trysil Ridge in English, it was named after the homeland community. Soon, the town was called "The Strip." And a post office/store was established. After the Soo Line Railroad came through, the residents petitioned to have the community named Rosewood, after the plentiful roses on the ridge.

Rosewood had a full complement of businesses, though not all at one time and many short-lived. They included a feed mill, cream station, a confectionary store that sold soft drinks, candy, and novelties and, for a time, lunches. A bank opened in 1920 but failed in 1927 costing many their life savings. The

dance hall was very popular. A large lumberyard, elevator, cement block factory, a café, a furniture store and a hardware store that offered barber services were also in the town. The general store was the longest lasting of them all.

The town was at its peak in 1915. With the advent of World War I, the town began its decline. The boys went off to war and the girls left for larger cities. The post office was discontinued in 1954.

Rosewood, 2014. (Courtesy of A. Filer)

Rosewood today. (Courtesy of A. Filer)

Mille Lacs County

The Opstead School. (Courtesy of Gerald Wollum)

The old Opstead church. (Courtesy of Gerald Wollum)

The John Skretting family. (Courtesy of Gerald Wollum)

LAWRENCE/POTTSTOWN

1890 - 1912

CLASS G

APPROXIMATE LOCATION:
East and west of Wahkon, absorbed by Wahkon

The three communities are in such close proximity that they not only share geographical boundaries but also share a common heritage and history. Lawrence was the first community in 1891, Pottstown in 1892 and when Wahkon was incorporated in 1912, it included both Lawrence and Pottstown.

First inhabited by Native Americans (Ojibwe) the area offered an abundance of natural resources the natives used extensively, including wild rice, maple syrup, blueberries, cranberries, fish, deer, and of course the many benefits of Mille Lacs Lake.

Don Robbins, a longtime Wahkon resident and area historian, wrote a book on the history of Wahkon. He also related the history of the towns in a recent telephone interview. According to Don, E.F. Sargeant was named the postmaster and named Lawrence, most likely after his hometown in Massachusetts.

In 1893, a stage coach line was established between Mora and Lawrence and was extended to Cove, the next community to the west. The stage stopped three times a week. By 1902, there were two stage lines to Lawrence. In 1894, Potts had a hotel and eating place in Lawrence. He sold that business in 1907. That building burned in 1910.

In 1901 Pottstown, just east of Lawrence was platted by T.E. Potts. Potts was an influential member of the area and had numerous connections and affiliations including the city council, school board, census taker, deputy assessor, and county commissioner.

Over time several businesses were established in Lawrence: a sawmill, real estate and law office, doctor, veterinarian, ice business, butcher shop, and saloon. Lawrence and Pottstown also had a school and several churches in the immediate area. Lawrence was in its heyday until 1917. The post office was moved from Lawrence to Wahkon in 1910.

When Wahkon was incorporated in 1912, the communities of Lawrence and Pottstown became part of Wahkon.

OPSTEAD

1889 – 1933 (1960s)

CLASS C

APPROXIMATE LOCATION:
1 mile from Isles on Minnesota #27/47, just past Becky Road

You could buy just about anything at Opstead's General Store. As an area resident wrote, the store carried everything from bullets to burlap and just about everything in between. If the store didn't carry it, you probably didn't need it. The store was perhaps the best known and most enduring aspect of the early Mille Lacs County community. The community's name was in honor of early settler John Skretting's home farm in Norway. John and Ellen Skretting and their two-year-old daughter arrived in the area in 1887. Most of the early settlers had originally settled in South Dakota and tried farming. Unsuccessful at long-term farming, they migrated to Minnesota, where the terrain was similar to that of their Scandinavian homeland. The dense woods provided work as loggers and the area's abundant wildlife supplemented their food supply, as did the region's berry growth.

There had been a Native American settlement in the area near Cedar Creek and today's Highway 18. In the mid-1880s, settlement was just beginning around the east side of Mille Lacs Lake with most of the newcomers arriving for logging. In 1892, a stage coach route was established between Aitkin and Opstead.

Opstead store, 1916. (Courtesy of Gerald Wollum)

As more and more settlers arrived, a school and church were needed. A Baptist Church was formed in 1891 and the Swedish Emmanuel Lutheran was formed in the early 1900s. The first school term was in 1893 and held in a private home. A school building was constructed and it stood where today's East Side Town Hall now stands.

In 1893, the first general store was built one-half mile south of Opstead's Corner (today's County Road #30). At that time there were no roads, no autos and no electricity. The store was located in the front with a kitchen and dining room in the back. A lean-to for storage was on the north side of the building as was a wood shed and chicken coop. In 1905 a building from Malmo was moved next to the store and was converted for use as a creamery. The creamery operated for two years. After its demise, the building was used as storage for the store. In the early days, the region's Native Americans would bring hand-sewn and beaded items in to trade for groceries.

A larger store was built in 1920 but before construction was completed, fire destroyed everything. Faulty wiring was thought to be the cause. Rebuilding began immediately. The store was said to carry the largest stock of goods of any store for miles around. Since it took nearly a day to get to Isle and back, the store carried groceries, clothing, sewing needs, building supplies, livestock needs, and even baby chicks. It was possible to special order many items including those from the Minnesota Farm Equipment line, which were manufactured by inmates at the Stillwater Prison. Many residents recall the glass cookie jars were displayed at just the right height for children to peer into.

A post office operated from 1899 to 1933. A local landmark was an eighty-five-foot flag pole. One early resident, Martin Skretting, even had a patent for a flag pole innovation. The flag was flown at half-mast when there was a death in the community or when a young man from the area went off to serve the nation.

In 1928, the store carried the Red and White grocery brand. Throughout the 1950s and 1960s, the store was a Greyhound Bus Station Stop. After many owners, the store closed in 1967 and stood vacant. It was torn down in 1972. The Baptist Church moved to the highway where it still stands today and is still very active.

Opstead lives on in memory, in name and in spirit. Opstead Junction and vicinity is still home to many.

Opstead store. (Courtesy of Gerald Wollum)

Morrison County

Early Holy Family Church. (Courtesy of Duane Welle/Holy Family)

Early convent. (Courtesy of Duane Welle/Holy Family)

Academy and convent today. (Author's collection)

BELLE PRAIRIE

1852 - 1904

CLASS A/H

APPROXIMATE LOCATION:
4 miles north of Little Falls on U.S. #371

Just north of Little Falls there is a scenic park along the banks of the Mississippi River. The park abounds in beauty, shaded respites, and history. I didn't know about the history of the area until I met Duane Welle. Welle, an area resident and local historian especially in all things Belle Prairie, has conducted extensive research on Belle Prairie, both the secular community and the nearby Belle Prairie/Holy Family site and its significant Christian history. More on the religious community later, first the history of Belle Prairie, the town.

Even before the town site was settled, a small trading post on a flat boat was established in 1826 in the area that would become Belle Prairie. Twenty years later, Frederick Ayer, the missionary, started the Protestant Congregational Church one mile north of today's Holy Family Church. He also established a mission and opened the first saw mill north of St. Anthony. It was Morrison County's first steam-powered sawmill. At one point, Ayers operated a missionary school for Native American children. However the school was later abandoned when the Native Americans were removed from the area. The settlement is one of the oldest in Northern Minnesota.

Ayer wasn't the only missionary in the area. In 1852 Father Pierz arrived. He established Belle Prairie as a mission, which was the first in the St. Cloud Diocese and only the second in all of Minnesota. That same year Ayer established a post office and was appointed postmaster. Records indicate that that mail was addressed "Belle Prairie, Upper Mississippi." The Red River Oxcart Trails ran through the settlement. Oftentimes the cart drivers would camp overnight in Belle Prairie as they were not welcomed in Little Falls because of the smell and noise they made. In 1856, St. Andrew's Church of Belle Prairie was established, it later became known as Holy Family.

In 1876, Chief Hole-In-The-Day threatened attacks in the area, so settlers moved to the Morrison County Courthouse for safety. They ended up staying for several weeks. They would work their fields during the day and return to the courthouse at night. A stagecoach also operated two routes through the community. One ran from St. Cloud to Little Falls, the other from Little Falls to Brainerd. A ferry across the river also operated in the mid-1870s. A rail station was established by the Western Railroad in 1877.

By the late 1800s, a railroad brochure description listed Belle Prairie's population at 800. It also listed that the community included a hotel, post office, stores, shops, a 10,000-bushel elevator, public hall, district schools, a Roman Catholic church, a convent and school, a lumberyard, general store, hotel, lodging houses, and several saloons. It should be kept in mind that the railroad description was written with the intent of enticing people to the area. Enhanced and often exaggerated descriptions were quite common and part of the marketing strategy.

Today there are no remains of Belle Prairie, the settlement. All that remains is the history, the legacy and the park at the

Holy Family and Academy. (Courtesy of Duane Welle)

Log cabin replica. (Courtesy of Duane Welle)

former town site. Whereas Belle Prairie's secular history was minimally recorded, Belle Prairie's Christian history and legacy are richly documented. Duane Welle, local historian of both Belle Prairie and Holy Family Church history, has shared some of his vast research and resources.

The first Mass in the region was conducted in 1838. In the 1840s Frederick Ayer established a mission and in 1852, Father Pierz arrived in Belle Prairie, establishing it as a mission site. St. Andrews Church of Belle Prairie was built in 1856. The name changed to Holy Family Church was in 1870.

In 1872, Mother Mary Ignatius Hays stepped off the stagecoach in Belle Prairie and her impact, her vision and her legacy have defined Belle Prairie since her arrival. Mother Ignatius Hays was by all accounts, a dynamo. She was focused, hard-driven, passionate and fervent in her beliefs and in her actions.

That same year of her arrival, 1872, Mother Hays opened a school. In 1873, several buildings were constructed including two boarding houses, a two-story dwelling house, a schoolhouse and a log cabin. Mother Hays fervently believed in her mission. She traveled to California in 1873 to solicit funds. She even had an audience with the pope where she laid out her plans and goals. A new church was built in 1877 to replace the original St. Andrew's/Holy Family Church building.

A new pastor arrived at Holy Family in 1878. He informed Mother Hays that she and the sisters could come to the Church for confession and communion. Undaunted she informed the pastor that he could come to them. Tensions between the two factions increased. A divided parish ensued. One night in 1889, a rider, dressed in black and mounted on a horse, rode by yelling, "The end is near." That night, a fire, simultaneously in two or three locations, started and the convent was burned to the ground. The fire destroyed everything but the log cabin used by Mother Hays in her first year in Belle Prairie. In the dark of the night, the sisters, many without their shoes, had to walk to Little Falls for shelter. The cause of the fire was determined to be arson.

In 1911, Mother Columbia Doucette rebuilt the school and named it "Our Lady of the Angels Academy." It was built on the site of the original convent. Through the years, the church and school grounds were expanded and renovated. Two wings were added to the building in 1930. A gymnasium was added in 1950, and in 1964 a new high school was constructed. During the summer of 1969, the sisters left Belle Prairie. With help from the diocese, the Holy Family Parish purchased the school property. The high school building is still used for religious education and other events. The former convent has been renovated to the Riverwood Pines Apartments.

Sacred memorial. (Author's collection)

Holy Family and Academy. (Author's collection)

118

The grounds of Holy Family are today a respite place and a must see. A historical marker briefly details the history of the area, Father Pierz's mission and more. Adjacent to the church is the Memorial Garden area. You can picnic under the shade trees, walk the flowered trails around the Stations of the Cross from the Our Lady of the Angels Academy and view the replica log cabin at the center of the site. A monument stands that hold the ashes of the tabernacle that were burned in the 1889 fire. The historic church is open daily for prayer, contemplation and to view the stunning stained glass windows. The entire complex is a faith-based legacy of the significant history of Belle Prairie.

CENTER VALLEY (ZERF)

Post Office 1910-1912

CLASS B

APPROXIMATE LOCATION:
From Pierz
East on County Highway 153 for approximately 5 miles
Turn right (south) on Partridge Road for approximately 4 miles. Near Creek

You can call it Zerf or you can call it Center Valley, either way you'd be right, for they are one and the same. Postal records indicate that Theo Billmeyer, the small community's founder, established two separate mail drops. One was dubbed Zerf, which was discontinued in 1902 and reestablished in 1910 as Center Valley, which lasted until 1912.

Aptly named, the community was located in the valley between two hills. Consisting of a few residences, a store with gas pumps, an ice house, a creamery and a sawmill. The store, minus its false front, was moved to the top of the hill along a busier county road (County 153) and is said to have operated until the 1970s and is reportedly still standing today serving as a private home.

The community was home to a creamery, known as the Clover Belt Creamery. In 1955, tragedy struck the creamery and the small community. When the boiler exploded, the buttermaker, Henry Marshik was severely injured. His clothing caught fire, and he had to jump into the nearby creek to extinguish the flames. Sadly, he died a few days later.

Marilyn Hesch Sebasky, who has family ties to the region, visited the old town site in 2009. She and another relative, in Marly's words "played archeologists" and went in search of Center Valley ruins. Maryls reports that some stone foundations are still visible, just off Partridge Road, on private property, behind the electric fence.

The Hesch family history website offers several photos and reminiscences of some of the community's residents. One memory, by Eddie Hiemez, recalls that, around 1940, Mr. Kinzer (the store owner) promised an ice-cream cone to anyone who could ride their bicycle up the hill without stopping. To Eddie's knowledge, no one every earned the cone.

While driving the rural roads in central Minnesota, near Merrifield, I came upon a roadside establishment with a large banner stating "Center Valley." What a coincidence, I knew it had to pertain to Morrison County's Center Valley. After doing a bit of research I located John Schmidtbauer, from the Center Valley area. John tells that when he started his band a few years back, he chose the name Center Valley in honor of the community.

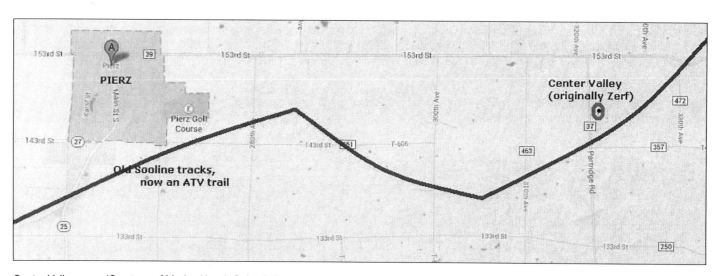

Center Valley map. (Courtesy of Marlys Hesch Sebasky)

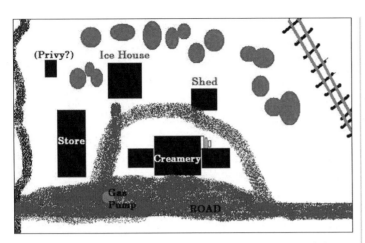

Center Valley possible layout. (Courtesy of Marlys Hesch Sebasky)

Center Valley store foundations. (Courtesy of Marlys Hesch Sebasky)

Center Valley store front. (Courtesy of Marlys Hesch Sebasky)

DARLING

1899 - 1908

CLASS C

APPROXIMATE LOCATION:
7 miles north of Little Falls on U.S. #10

I have never seen the Darling train depot. In fact, I have never seen a photo of it. So when I came upon John Cartwright's website, www.artrail.com, I was fascinated. John has created pencil drawings of hundreds of train stations and depots, many no longer existing. Using old photographs,

Center Valley store front. (Courtesy of Marlys Hesch Sebasky)

Darling station sketch. (Courtesy of John Cartwright www.artrail.com)

many taken by himself as a youngster, old books and other resources, he has created a look into the past that all of us can relate to. Many of the ink drawings are of lost towns, others are towns and cities we all know of, but often the train depots are long gone. Check it out, you'll be transported back to the old train days of lore, and everyone will know a town or several that are featured on John's artwork.

LITTLE ELK

Mid 1850s

CLASS A

APPROXIMATE LOCATION:
1½ mile north of Little Falls at the mouth of the Little Elk River

Today when Little Elk is discussed it is most often in terms of the archeological excavating and the early prehistory settlement as well as the historic preservation.

In its earliest days Little Elk was the site of an early Native American village.

During the Mission settlement time, approximately 1858, the area, with its water supply and power was home to a dam, sawmill, and flour mill. Just before and after the Civil War, the areas businesses faded and eventually died out. In approximately 1884, Alfred Tanner sold his mill at Swan River and moved his machinery to Little Elk. It was said to produce fifty barrels a day.

Ashby Morrill also ran a large sawmill and rebuilt the flour mill. He also had a large mansion built in 1892. Nothing but the best was used in the construction and furnishing of the mansion. Materials came from all over the world and included works of art. The grounds included a large stable and housing for the many servants, including stablemen, butlers, and maids.

When Major Morrill died, the home and site declined rapidly especially during the Depression years of the twentieth century. In 1976 all that remained were stone abutments at the main gate and bricks and stones near the cellar. Today the site is a protected archeological site. For five weeks each summer students and archeologists conduct digs and studies and continue to uncover the rich history of the site.

VAWTER

1908 - 1940

CLASS A

APPROXIMATE LOCATION:
2 miles east of Highway #10 on Morrison County Road #34
(Buckman Road)

According to local folklore, Vawter was located in the worst swamp land anywhere. The area was so wet and water-logged that frustrated residents threw up their hands muttering, "Vawter, Vawter, everywhere." Thus the community's name.

The town, platted in 1908, had twelve blocks of various sized lots. Most of the town was south of the railroad tracks. Avenues ran east and west and Main Street ran north and south. Street names included Lamb, Thomas, and Palona. Lamb was one of the original storekeepers. The community included a general store and a post office from 1922 to 1940. The Central Livestock Association used the area as a hub to ship thousands of livestock throughout the United States. In 1922, the Association moved to nearby Royalton.

Otter Tail County

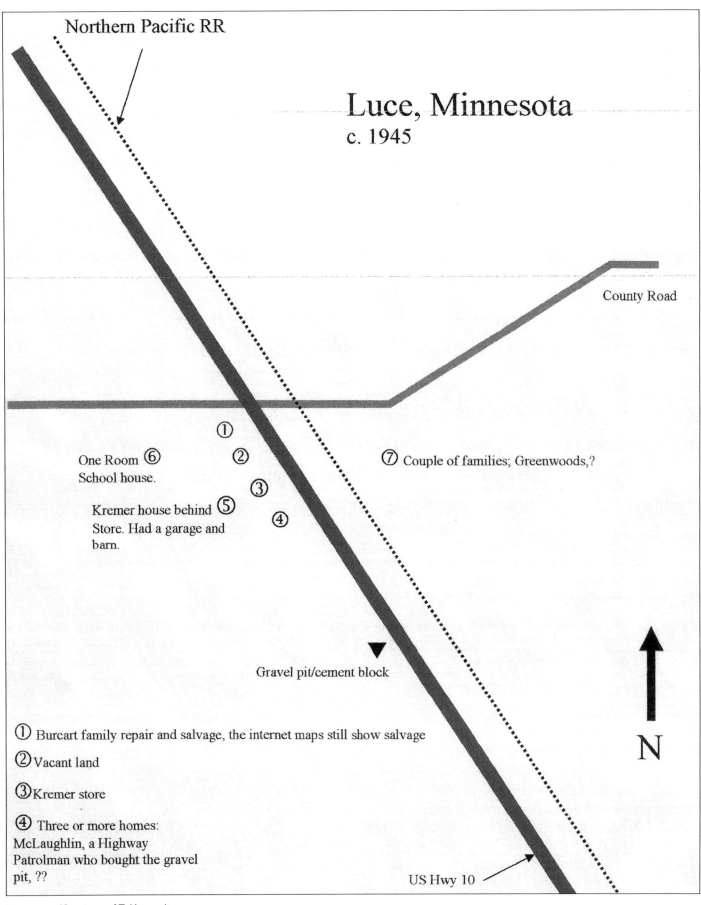

Northern Pacific RR

Luce, Minnesota
c. 1945

County Road

①

One Room ⑥
School house.

②

⑦ Couple of families; Greenwoods,?

③

Kremer house behind ⑤
Store. Had a garage and
barn.

④

▼
Gravel pit/cement block

N

① Burcart family repair and salvage, the internet maps still show salvage

② Vacant land

③ Kremer store

④ Three or more homes:
McLaughlin, a Highway
Patrolman who bought the gravel
pit, ??

US Hwy 10

Luce map. (Courtesy of T. Kremer)

BUTLER

1897 - 1954

CLASS A

APPROXIMATE LOCATION:
Highway 148 southwest of Menahga just west of Highway 67

Traveling to Holland in 1908, Reverend Vanden Heuvel was quite the salesman. Hired and financed by a land development company, the reverend was sent to urge his fellow Dutchmen to purchase land in Otter Tail County Minnesota. Offering prime land (at least the advertising touted it as prime) at thirty dollars an acre (the developers paid only two dollars an acre), the deals were too good to pass up. Over 200 purchased land, in sixty-acre minimums and ventured to start a new life in Minnesota.

Arriving in Minnesota and seeing first-hand the land they had purchased, the immigrants were disappointed. The fertile farmland they had been promised turned out to be swamp land. Conditions were crude and harsh, at best. One family arriving in Otter Tail County with her parents recalls that upon arrival they had to board on the top floor of the store. Besieged by hordes of unknown bugs that bit (they turned out to be bed bugs), she never forgot the incident.

The community was named for an early Otter Tail County treasurer, Stephen Butler. A post office operated from 1897 until 1954 and later as a rural branch until 1957. Primary businesses were a township hall, a store, and a cheese factory.

Times were hard. A 1914 scarlet fever epidemic decimated the community. Folks did what they could to eke out a living. Trapping was of great importance in the early years. Weasels earned $4.00 to $6.00 each and were often the only income available.

The young girl who always remembered the bed bugs also recalled her family's onion crop. Knowing that onions were very expensive in Rotterdam, their home, the family planted two acres of them. When harvest time came, they took the onions to Perham sure they were going to make a good profit. They sold nary a one. Disappointed they returned home and dumped the onions in a corner of the barn. The nearly starving cows devoured them, which in turn tainted the milk. Thus they could not sell the cream.

Most of the Dutch were city people and could not adapt to the farming, especially in the poor, swampy land. However, there were good times, and the community spirit was always thriving. Remnants of the community lasted until the late twentieth century. The regional name still lives on as well as in the township name. The memories live on as well in the hearts and minds of those who called Butler home.

LUCE

1883 - 1948

CLASS C

APPROXIMATE LOCATION:
Near intersection of U.S. Highway 10 and County Roads #60 and #228

One of the town's I'm most often asked about is Luce in Otter Tail County. The once-thriving community was home the "First and Last Chance Saloon" and several other businesses. Most of the town was lost when U.S. Highway 10 was widened. Yet there are many who have fond memories of Luce in its day.

The Kremer family is one family with ties and memories of Luce. The Luce Post Office operated from 1883 until 1948. For the last three years, 1945 to 1948, the postmaster was the Kremer boy's father. Kremer was recently returned to the area from World War II in September of 1944 in a POW exchange. One son recalls a one-room schoolhouse. He later rode the Greyhound Bus to Perham to attend school.

The community had a store/post office combination. Nothing elaborate, the post office was a small section in the west rear of the building, with a cubby-hole system of mail boxes. There was a small area in the front of the store with tables and chairs. Barrels of pickles, herring, crackers, and other delicacies were nearby. A small cooler dispensed beer and pop. There was a large walk-in cooler in back that held meat. There was also a small area for cutting and wrapping the meat. Clothing was along the west wall.

On the west side of the store's exterior was another small building and gas pump. The gas pump wasn't used very often and was most likely for kerosene. The area between the house and the store was a vacant area of about 150 feet. A small street ran between the store and the other houses, past the Kremer house, the school and out to the highway leading to Vergas. Memories sure can paint a vivid picture.

OLD CLITHERALL
1865 - EARLY 1900s

CLASS C

APPROXIMATE LOCATION:
North shore of Lake Clitherall, Highway #210 and 402nd Avenue (Clitherall Lake Road)

Traveling by covered wagon from Iowa, the seven families and forty-one people, headed towards north central Minnesota in search of a new homestead. All were

Clitherall Depot. (Author's Collection)

Clitherall Store, 2007. (Courtesy of Perry Exley)

Clitherall Garage, 2007. (Courtesy of Perry Exley)

Clitherall house, 2007. (Courtesy of Perry Exley)

members of a branch of the Latter Day Saints known as the Cutlerites. Their founder, Father Cutler had prophesized that they should "settle on the land between two lakes." Coming upon Otter Tail County's Clitherall Lake area, they knew this was to be their new home. The lake was named for George Clitherall, a land office surveyor in Otter Tail County from 1858 to 1861 The new settlement took its name from the lake and was Otter Tail County's earliest white settlement. Not only was it the earliest settlement, Clitherall was the first township, the first school district, and the county's first auditor, the first two county school superintendents and two members of the first Board of County Commissioners came from Clitherall.

The new settlers were hardy and took to establishing their new homesteads immediately. Each settler had a trade (shoemaker, carpenter, loomers, even a photographer). The first winter was harsh. The closest post office was one hundred miles away in St. Cloud and the nearest trade center was sixty-five miles away in Sauk Centre. They did have cook stoves but no heating stoves that first year. One early resident recalled that the bread froze so hard overnight that it had to be cut with an axe the next morning. The following year, heating stoves were used.

The town grew rapidly and some sources record that, at one time, over forty buildings were in the settlement.

The homesteaders had been warned that just a few years before their arrival, Minnesota had been in the grips of the Dakota Conflict. The settlers had no problem with the area's natives and in fact had a friendly relationship with them. They also had friendly and amiable relations with other settlers in the area.

Their religion was a driving, ever-present force in their lives and from the first day they arrived, they held services. The services were held first outdoors, and then in homes until a log church was built in 1870. A wood-frame building was erected in 1912.

School was held every weekday except for Monday, which was washday. School books were carried from Iowa.

A large Fourth of July celebration was held each year for many years. People from miles around joined the festivities.

126

Clitherall cemetery. (Courtesy of Perry Exley)

The Declaration of Independence was read. Long tables of every food imaginable were offered and one resident, after forty-eight years still recalled the gooseberry pies.

One winter Wednesday the weather was ideal, temps were mild and the winds were calm. A few flakes started falling, the wind picked up and before long folks out and about couldn't see a foot in front of them. They scarcely reached their destinations. Residents said they hadn't seen such a storm in fifty years. The storm raged for three days and nights.

In 1877 the settlers had a bountiful wheat crop, until the grasshoppers moved in. One summer day around noon, a black cloud of locusts swarmed in. They began eating everything in sight. After devouring everything, they laid their eggs and moved on. The results were devastating. One local farmer recorded that his entire harvest that year was eighteen bushels. Because of the eggs there was no harvest the following year and the settlers experienced extreme hardship.

The railroad came to the area in 1881 and the line ran approximately two miles from the settlement. The area around the tracks grew and developed. People and businesses began

Clitherall cemetery. (Courtesy of Perry Exley)

Clitherall pump. (Courtesy of Perry Exley)

Clitherall cornerstone. (Courtesy of Perry Exley)

Old Clitherall church, 2007. (Courtesy of Perry Exley)

to move to the new site, which became known as Clitherall while the old settlement became "Old Clitherall." Old Clitherall struggled to survive. Eventually the settlement declined. The remaining Cluterites moved to Independence, Missouri, where the Church's branch headquarters were located. Most buildings were moved or torn down.

According to the Old Town Resort website, the property was bought by the Lord family from Breckenridge, Minnesota, in the 1930s. It was used as a summer retreat for a sick child. The child was never sick again. In the 1940s several cabins were built and the property was used as a summer resort. Ione Lord Nelson, the once sick child, owned it until 1974. Cabin 7 was the old school house and Otter Tail County's first school. It was later moved along the shore in the 1950s. The old church building still stands and is cared for by descendants of the first settlers.

The old general store stood vacant for over thirty years. In 2013, the building was restored and is now "Justice Two." It is a unique and historical must see. Espresso drinks, sandwiches, ice cream, treats, candy, groceries and more are offered. The second floor is a meeting space with a pool table, foosball table and dartboard.

Pine County

Boston Corbett. (Author's collection)

BELDEN

1897 - 1954

CLASS A

APPROXIMATE LOCATION:
East of Minnesota/Wisconsin Border, along abandoned rail
tracks now the Gandy Dancer Trail, Nemadji State Forest

Always a lumber and pulpwood settlement, swamp land surrounded Belden. The town was incorporated in 1921 and dissolved in 1943. Named for a land office worker in Minneapolis, the Soo Line ran its tracks through the area in 1912. Though the land was poor for farming, there was lots of timber in the region. The business district included a store/post office, a blacksmith with three forges, hotel, an over-size boarding house, and a railroad depot, which hosted several community events and church services. A school for the loggers' children was built in 1916 and operated until 1939 when it was sold and demolished. The town survived as long as the timber did. With poor land, war, and fires, the loss of the timber resources signaled the decline and demise of Belden.

By 1943, the once thriving community of Belden was abandoned. Since the late 1930s, all that remained was a collection of vacant buildings. One of the buildings was a large barn, said to be the largest in Pine County at the time. It could hold over fifty horses. Another building, the general store, had closed in 1938 and was still fully stocked. The sole owner decided to sell the town, property, buildings and contents by public auction.

On a cold November day, over two hundred and fifty attended the auction sale to disperse of the town and all its remnants. The blacksmith shop, complete with all the tools and equipment went first. Selling for $300, the big barn was next on the block. The loggers shacks were sold after that, one at a time, with the deer hunters being evicted as each was sold. Last was the store and all its goods. With thousands upon thousands of small items, including food still in the tins, bolts of fabric, clothing, notions, and more, the store was sold in bits at ten dollars a shelf. By the end of the day, Belden and everything in it was sold to the highest bidder.

The railroad line to Belden was abandoned and the track pulled up. Today the grade is the Gandy Dancer Trail and is used for recreational purposes in the Nemadji State Forest.

CLOVERDALE

1890s – 1960s

CLASS C

APPROXIMATE LOCATION:
Intersection of Highway 48 and Pine County #21

Without definitive proof, we may never know what happened to Thomas "Boston" Corbett. Known as the man who shot and killed John Wilkes Booth, the assassin of President Abraham Lincoln, Corbett's life was tragic, at least through his later years.

Corbett, born in London, England, in 1832, later moved to America. A hatter by trade, which may have been a cause of his later mental problems, as hatters worked with lead and lead poisoning was a leading cause of mental issues. Always considered "different and a religious fanatic," Corbett joined the Union Army at the onset of the Civil War. Re-enlisting three times, he was one of twenty-six men chosen to pursue Booth after the assassination of Lincoln. Cornering the accused assassin in a barn, the soldiers set the barn on fire. Corbett, spotting Booth through a large crack in the barn wall, shot him at close range. Corbett dragged Booth's body from the barn. Booth's spinal cord had been severed by the bullet, and he died shortly thereafter. Corbett was placed under technical arrest until the charges were later dropped. A reward of $1,653.85 was awarded to Corbett.

After the war, Corbett returned to being a hatter. In 1878 he moved to Kansas where he lived in a dug-out. In 1887, he was appointed the assistant doorkeeper of the Kansas House of Representatives. Often paranoid, one day Corbett pulled out his pistol and held members of the House hostage. He was arrested, declared insane and sent to the Topeka Asylum for the Insane.

How does this tie in to Cloverdale, Minnesota? In 1887 Corbett escaped from the asylum. Historians, including Bill O'Reilly in *Killing Lincoln*, speculate that Corbett made his way to Minnesota, near Cloverdale, where he lived for several years. He is believed to have perished in the 1894 Great Hinckley Fire. While there is no definitive proof, a Thomas Corbett is listed among the dead and missing.

Cloverdale, the town, was originally called Turpville, because of the area's turpentine industry. Begun by Russian immigrants, the Copilovich brothers, familiar with the distilling process, the Standard Turpentine Company extracted pine tar and oil of tar from Norway pine stumps. The cut-over, sandy soil of the region made for an abundance of tree stumps. Farmers brought the stumps into the plant where four extractors pulled tar from them, and tanks held the tar to be made into turpentine. The industry lasted as long as the stumps did, which, by varying estimates, was three to seven years, primarily from 1903 to 1909. The community's name was changed to Cloverdale, in deference to the area's wild and cultivated clover.

The Cloverdale Cooperative Creamery/Land O'Lakes was active from 1921 to 1946. Farmers separated the milk on their farms, then brought the cream into the creamery to be churned into butter. In 1946, cream began to be hauled to a larger, centrally located plant in Hinckley. The Cloverdale creamery, its equipment and its assets were sold at public auction. A farm supply and repair service was built on the creamery site. A New Holland/Rambler Automobile dealership was also part of the community. Other town staples were the Cloverdale Garage, the Dewey Avenue Bar, and the Cloverdale Store. Cholette's Corner was an area landmark since the late 1920s. A Grange was active for many years as was Steen Park.

The area had three schools. The early Turpville School was in disrepair but still stood in the early 2000s. It was/is located on Minnesota #48, three quarters of a mile from Cloverdale. It ceased operation as a school in 1969.

CLOVERTON

1917 – 1970s

CLASS A

APPROXIMATE LOCATION:
Just west of the Minnesota/Wisconsin border at the junction of County Roads #32 and #31

Based on a lumber and pulpwood economy, the area was settled when the Soo Line Railroad came through Pine County, and the lands were opened up for homesteading. Potatoes and red clover were the principle farm crops, and it was the region's abundant clover that gave Cloverton its name. Upham writes that, in 1916, half of the township was owned by the Red Clover Land Company headquartered in Iowa.

A school district was organized in 1917 and the first school, a two-room wood-frame building was erected. When the original building burned to the ground in 1918, it was replaced with a brick building. Said to be a showplace, the school served 165 students and employed seven teachers. Records indicate that the

Cloverton School. (Courtesy of Pinecountyhistory.blogspot.com)

Cloverton school today. (Common use)

school served hot lunches thirty years before it became the norm elsewhere. Twelve grades were taught and French was part of the curriculum. The high school program ended in 1946, and by the 1960s the elementary grades were discontinued. In 1980, the brick school building was placed on the National Register of Historic Places and was later used as an apartment building. The building has since been demolished.

The decline of Cloverton was the result of the poor farm economy along with the dwindling timber resources. A 1923 fire that swept through the area destroyed nearly a dozen Cloverton buildings. Residents fled to the brick school for safety. The burned buildings were never rebuilt.

Community events were common and well-attended. Two of the most popular were the Independence Day celebration, which featured a pot-luck meal. Pot luck was also a key component of the annual Christmas program as was Santa and treats for all of the children.

Cloverton Early Contractor. (Courtesy of Pinecountyhistory.blogspot.com)

ELLSON

1904 - 1925

CLASS A

APPROXIMATE LOCATION:
County Highway #41 just east of Maple Road

Slated to be called "Bremen," Elway Ellson signed the town documents on the wrong line, thus the name of the small community was recorded as "Ellson."

The community's primary business was the Halfway House, so named because of its halfway location between Willow River and Aitkin County's White Pine village. The long two-story, wood-framed, store-fronted building had cooking and lodging facilities for twelve travelers. It also served as a general store and post office. A township hall, school house, and a small number of homes completed the community.

On October 12, 1918, the town and the Ellson buildings were destroyed by the Moose Lake Fire. Residents recalled that roofs were dowsed with water to keep them from burning. One woman, a child at the time of the fire, remembered that her family, in fear of losing their home, carried all of their possessions to the potato field. As fate would have it, the house was spared and all of their worldly possessions in the potato field were lost to the fire.

Dwindling timber resources, poor farm land, fires, and the economy all contributed to Ellson's demise.

GREELEY

1886 - 1902

CLASS A

APPROXIMATE LOCATION:
Royalton Township

A creamery was started in 1901 and was said to have the best equipment available at the time. The Royal Creamery, as it was called, had 134 patrons in 1939. It closed in the 1960s, and the building was converted into a private home. A general store was also located in Greeley. Nothing remains today.

Kingsdale railroad depot. (Courtesy of J. Burt, www.west2k.com)

KINGSDALE

1911 - 1961

CLASS A

APPROXIMATE LOCATION:
Just west of the Minnesota/Wisconsin border at intersection of County Highways #31 and Kingsdale

When the Soo Line Railroad came through the area in 1911, it brought loggers and their families to the region. One of the first buildings constructed in the new community was a hotel and store, built by C.R. Grace on his land. Shortly after the loggers arrived, a school was build and was used not only for school functions but for community events as well. By 1919, the community of Kingsdale included two stores, two sawmills, a lumberyard, a general store, a hardware, a restaurant, a barber shop, and the large Grace Hotel. The hotel provided accommodations for the working men, traveling salesmen, and the pulpwood and potato buyers who frequently visited the community.

A Presbyterian Church was active for over fifty years but, in 1968, as membership declined the congregation was dissolved. The church building was then used as the township hall. The school closed in 1938, and the building was sold and torn down. With the decline of the area's timber resources, the community declined. Eventually all of the buildings were burned or razed. The former train depot collapsed in 2014.

Markville. (Courtesy of Pinecountyhistory.blogspot.com)

MARKVILLE

1890 - 1931

CLASS A

APPROXIMATE LOCATION:
Just west of the Minnesota/Wisconsin border at intersection of County Highways 25 (Markville Road) and #31.

Markville was once one of Pine County's fastest growing communities, Markville was an offshoot of Pansey, a Wisconsin trade center and site of a crude ferry crossing. Mark Andrews, of Pansy, platted the town shortly before the railroad came in 1911, and named it after himself.

Settled in 1905, the Red Clover Company owned 28,000 acres of land. They conducted extensive advertising for settlers. When the Soo Line arrived in 1911, the site, which had a sawmill built in the 1890s, grew quickly. Home to two sawmills, two grocery stores, a bank, a garage, two restaurants, a hotel, a creamery, blacksmith, lumberyard, pool hall, and several homes, the town was booming and was officially organized in 1917. The community also had a newspaper, *The Union Enterprise*.

A one-room school joined the community and the original school building was later occupied by the area's Lutheran Church. In 1917, a brick school building was erected—bricks on three sides, with a tarpaper back wall. In 1918 the population of Markville was 250. In 1920 to 1925 there were 100 students with five teachers. The high school grades were discontinued during the Depression and the grade school closed in the 1960s. The building was razed in the 1970s and the materials were used to build a garage.

The citizens of Markville were community minded from the beginning. A community club promoted better schools, better roads, better farming practices, and better health and recreation. One of their annual events was a community fair. Other active groups included the Boy Scouts, 4-H, and a women's group called the "Sunshine Club." The community's three churches also played an active role in town life.

As the timber resources dwindled, so did Markville, eventually declining and fading into history. A reunion was held in 1961, and over 600 people attended.

MILBURN

Late 1890s

CLASS A

APPROXIMATE LOCATION:
East of Pine City, 1 mile north of County Road #8 on
Cemetery Road

An early disaster in the area was commemorated in the village's name. A mill built in 1892-1893 was completely destroyed by fire the same day the Great Hinckley Fire raged through the area in September of 1894, thus the name "Milburn."

Early immigrants from Sweden settled the area. The community had two churches, both on the St. Croix Road. One was a Norwegian Lutheran Church and the other the Swedish Free Mission Church.

The Milburn (Enger) School was closed in 1970. It was still standing in the late 1970s but in disrepair. Little else is known about the community.

POKEGAMA

1900 – 1918 (1940s)

CLASS A/C

APPROXIMATE LOCATION:
Pine County Roads #7 and #13

Pokegama is the name for many places and locations within Pine County. Records indicate it was originally the site of an Ojibwe village on the shores of Pokegama Lake, the village once housed a mission operated by Frederick Ayer. The mission is reputed to have printed the first Christian Bible in the Ojibwe Language.

Other records indicate that the settlement was once a logging camp that developed into a community. In the early hours of the Great Hinckley Fire, the residents of Pokegama fled to a pool or water in the creek for safety and to escape the flames. Everyone in the water survived, but all suffered burns. Though spared their lives, the survivors lost everything. Pokegama was completely destroyed. The tragic news spread world-wide, and donations from all over the United States and Europe flooded in. The settlement was rebuilt and is now known as Brook Park.

A few historical resources document a nearby tuberculosis sanitorium in Pokegama. Operating on a thirty-five-acre site

Pokegama Sanitorium postcard. (Author's collection)

near Pokegama lake, the hospital could house thirty-six patients. In use as a tuberculosis center from 1905 until 1943, the building was later sold to the Catholic Church. It was used as an administration center, retirement home and priesthood school. The Church later left the building. Parts of the 1918 building were also used for a short time as a chemical addiction treatment center. It was abandoned in 1986 and was still standing in the early twenty-first century.

Sanitorium. (Couresty of Dan Turner, www.substreet.org)

Sanitorium today. (Couresty of Dan Turner, www.substreet.org)

WEST ROCK

1870s

CLASS A

APPROXIMATE LOCATION:
Near the intersection of Pine County #70 and #103

Named on the quick when a resident needed an address for a pay phone installation, the West Rock community consisted of a school, store, creamery, and a church. The church, built in 1890, began as a Presbyterian Church and later converted to a Lutheran Church. Little else is known about the community.

Roseau County

Casperson. (Courtesy of A. Filer)

Haug. (Courtesy of A. Filer)

BENWOOD

1904 - 1925

CLASS A

APPROXIMATE LOCATION:
150th Street between 310th Avenue and 320th Avenue,
Poplar Grove Township

Being an inland town has its logistical issues. Without nearby railroad service, all supplies and store merchandise has to be freighted in, by horse and wagon. In the early days, mail was delivered once a week from Strathcona. A post office did operate in Benwood from 1904 to 1925. A general store was also in the community.

Settled by Norwegian Lutherans, the town site was situated between two ridges, the Klondike to the east and the Siberian to the west.

CASPERSON

1903 - 1917

CLASS A

APPROXIMATE LOCATION:
Golden Valley Township

Casperson was named for two brothers who homesteaded in the area. A post office operated from 1903 to 1917.

HAUG

1897 - 1932

CLASS C

APPROXIMATE LOCATION:
West of Roseau, Solar Township, near intersection of Roseau
County Roads #7 and 290th Street

The small Norwegian community had a post office from 1897 until 1931. In 1901, area residents established the Midland Norwegian Evangelical Church, also called the Haug Church. In 1901 there were thirty-seven members, by 1915 membership was down to fifteen and in the 1920s, the church was closed. A store, filling station, and telephone office were also part of the community.

MALUNG

1895 - 1954

CLASS D

APPROXIMATE LOCATION:
Roseau County Road #2 and Malung Street

Deciding that the best way to retain their Swedish identity in their new country, the Swedish immigrants and first postmaster named their new community after their old, Malung, which was in the west central area of Dalecarlia, Sweden.

The town was platted in 1897, but a school pre-dated the town's official formation. The first school building, in 1894 was in the home of an early settler, who lived with his wife and three daughters in the upstairs. The school teacher earned $130 a month and lived right in the school room. The second school was in an area bachelor's house.

When platted, Malung was comprised of five blocks, a Main Street, a Malung Avenue, and an alley. In 1898, blocks 1, 2 and 5 were sold to the Malung Manufacturing Company, though no one remembers and records don't tell just what they manufactured. One lot was also sold to the school district. Over the years, as the school expanded, additional lots were sold to the school district. When the school consolidated, the buildings were sold and moved.

The residents of Malung were hard-working and community-minded. A Good Templars organization was established, and they sponsored many community events and celebrations including annual Christmas programs. The building was later sold and moved to Ross. A two-day celebration, called Dalfohert, honoring Swedish culture and folklore was held each year for decades.

Malung. (Courtesy of A. Filer)

A post office operated from 1895 to 1954. Originally part of Kittson County, the post office building was later moved to Roseau and used as a family home.

The Roseau County Press was published for a short time in Malung. The newspapers founder and others believed Malung sat on rich oil deposits. A device called a "magnometer" was invented, and its purpose was to located oil reserves. Nothing was ever found. The community also had high hopes the Great Northern Railroad would come through their town, but it never did and as such, the community began its decline.

MANDUS

1911 - 1913

CLASS A

APPROXIMATE LOCATION:
Spruce Township four miles east of Roseau

Formerly called Lucan, the small community of Mandus had a short-lived post office as well as a store and railroad stop. Area farmers would drop off their cream and eggs at the railroad station, known as "The Boxcar" for shipment to Warroad and Roseau. The community was named for Mandus Erickson, owner of the store.

PENTUREN

1908 - 1937

CLASS A/C

APPROXIMATE LOCATION:
Beltrami Island State Forest, off Summer Forest Road

Open twenty-four hours a day, seven days a week, the Penturen Church welcomes everyone who stops by. Also known as the "Cathederal in the Pines" visitors are encouraged to step inside, sign the guest book, read about the church's history and partake in prayer, or search for a geocache on the grounds. Tinkling wind-chimes add to the serenity of the site.

The church originated in 1926, has been restored and is located in the Beltrami Island State Forest. The church was once part of the community of Penturen, which had a post office from 1908 until 1937. The town was settled in three different locations in Elkwood Township, in sections 29, 32 and 36, all along the Roseau River. The early 1900s saw a land boom in the area. The peatlands were ditched and drained to be used for agricultural purposes but the sandy, swampy land made farming next to impossible. President Roosevelt's New Deal programs, specifically the Resettlement Administration, as-

Mandus. (Courtesy of A. Filer)

Interior Penturen church. (Courtesy of T. Kremer)

Exterior Penturen church. (Courtesy of T. Kremer)

Penturen church. (Courtesy of T. Kremer)

sisted area residents in relocating during the 1930s, virtually abandoning homesteads and communities.

The state forest, which now encompasses the old town site of Penturen as well as several other lost towns in the region, was established in 1933. Its 700,000-plus acres offers a glimpse into the past with historical markers placed at sites throughout the forest. There are designated scenic and historic drives. The region is a destination for recreational opportunities.

Ross

1890 - 1892

CLASS C

APPROXIMATE LOCATION:
Near junction of MN #89 and Roseau County #10

The original town site of Ross was one-half mile west of the present site. The community had a post office (1890 to 1892), a school, town hall, creamery, and a store. Little else is known about the settlement.

Salol

1907 - 1993

CLASS D

APPROXIMATE LOCATION:
12 Miles from Warroad on MN #11

When it came time to name the Roseau County town, L. Dahlquist, a drug store clerk and later county superintendent, scanned the labels of on the bottles of medicines on the shelf. Submitting several names, the post office approved "Salol" in 1907, and thus the community was named for the white powder used as a remedy for rheumatism and neuralgia.

The area's rich timber resources offered promising growth. Many believed the area would become a metropolis. Most of the region's settlers were from Vetbotten, Sweden. Early settlement was difficult at best, as the roads to the region were nearly impossible to navigate. When the railroad came to the region, settlement boomed, and lumber became big business. Cedar posts and tamarack ties were shipped out by the rail cars. The community grew. Salol soon had a bank, two hotels, a store/post office, tailor shop, and general store.

The year 1910 was especially dry, and the region was in severe drought. A peat fire began on October 9, 1910, and swept through the area. Baudette and Spooner got the worst of the fire. Salol was aided by a special train helping with evacuation. The train's whistle blew continuously so people could find it in the thick, heavy smoke. Luckily there was no loss of life in Salol. The school was destroyed, but the state did pay $800 towards the cost of replacing the building.

A Good Templar Hall was built in 1916 and in 1917 was joined by a Yeoman's Lodge. By 1926 the abundant timber supply was in decline. Most businesses in Salol closed or moved, and the area became an agricultural-based region. In recent years, due to the employment opportunities provided by Marvin Windows and Polaris Industries, a resurgence has taken place.

Ross today. (Courtesy of A. Filer)

Salol Store. (Courtesy of A. Filer)

Salol today. (Courtesy of A. Filer)

SKIME

1910 - 1960

CLASS C

APPROXIMATE LOCATION:
14 Miles from Wannaska on Roseau County #9

Operating under a succession of owners, the Skime Store was built in 1909 by Alfred Skime, a bachelor settler. A post office was established in 1910 and operated for fifty years, closing in 1960. It then operated as rural branch until 1964. When Alfred married in 1917, he sold the store and through the years, several owners ran the business. The Reine Town Hall and school were also in the community. In later years cabins were rented for area visitors.

Skime store. (Courtesy of A. Filer)

Skime today. (Courtesy of A. Filer)

Skime. (Courtesy of A. Filer)

SWIFT

1905 - 1985

CLASS C

APPROXIMATE LOCATION:
5 Miles southwest of Warroad on MN #11

Once a station stop along the Canadian National Railroad, it was the train that gave the community its name, actually, both of its names. Originally called

Muirhead Siding, the tale goes that one day, early settlers Muirhead and others watched the train speed through the area. They marveled at how "swift" it was, thus the town's name. Due to the extensive logging in the area, Swift had several sawmills in the region. A post office operated from 1905 to 1985. The community also included several stores, a hotel, a pool room, blacksmith, and feed barn.

Swift today. (Courtesy of A. Filer)

Swift today. (Courtesy of A. Filer)

St. Louis County

Buchanan shoreline. (Author's collection)

Lake Superior at Buchanan. (Author's collection)

BUCHANAN

1856 -1862

CLASS A/G

APPROXIMATE LOCATION:
Immediately west of Knife River Minnesota on Highway #61
- Historical Marker

Minnesota's North Shore Drive is one of the most scenic routes anywhere on earth. With panoramic views, breath-taking vistas, and stunning sights, it is a feast for the eyes. Dozens of roadside pullouts offer respite for the traveler, including postcard picture shots of rocky shoreline, sparkling water, and wooded landscapes and unparalleled beauty. One such stop, immediately west of the small community of Knife River is my favorite. Known as the Buchanan Wayside, the pullover features a historical marker depicting the brief history of the long-ago settlement of Buchanan. The wayside was removed from the Minnesota Department of Transportation's jurisdiction in 1965 and fell into a bit of disrepair. However, when I visited in 2014, it was evident the wayside had been renovated and now resembles a park.

As for the marker and the history of Buchanan, the brief history offers a glimpse into the long ago settlement. Buchanan was a short-lived venture that, for a brief time, played a significant role in the development of Northeastern Minnesota. Early laws dictated that each of Minnesota's six land districts have a land office staffed by federal employees. Land office responsibilities included recording all transactions and payments and settling disputes. The Northeastern Minnesota district encompassed all lands ceded in the 1854 LaPointe Treaty. In 1856, Buchanan, named for then U.S. president, included 315 acres. It was subdivided into four-hundred-by-one-hundred-fifty-foot blocks and lots. Streets were eighty feet in width and paralleled the lake. Closest to the shoreline, was Lake Street, the others were numbered First through Fourteenth and the avenues were named for area geographical

Buchanan wayside. (Author's collection)

151

stones (Feldspar, Granite, etc). Land sales and development were expected to be brisk especially since the area had long been rumored to have copper deposits. Small amounts had been found and it was believed larger veins existed.

The land office was slow in getting established. In 1857, it was reported that improvements were being completed. In addition to the land office, the settlement included one hotel, a boarding house, several taverns and a few homes. Nearly all were constructed of logs. Records indicate that the streets were nothing more than mud paths and trails. Buchanan did have a substantial pier and dock on the lake. In 1858, the Minnesota legislature authorized incorporation of the town (township) of Buchanan.

Buchanan had several factors working against its success: a nationwide economic downturn and depression in 1857, political partisanship, and the realization that, against hope, there were no copper deposits. In June of 1858, amid complicated political maneuverings and a politically charged atmosphere, the land office was moved to Duluth. Within a short time the town site of Buchanan was abandoned and was being rapidly reclaimed by nature. The first fatality was, due to spring breakup, the pier and dock. Cabins were vacant and empty. Buildings were razed by forest fires. Nature reclaimed the area so quickly that it was impossible to determine the exact location of the buildings and land office.

According to a 1991 *Minnesota History* article by Glenn Sandvick, some questioned whether Buchanan had existed at all, saying it had been a "paper town" only. Sandvick writes that primary source documents including one that had one of the pioneer mining Merritt brother's calling Buchanan "the Emporium of the North Shore," soundly dispute the paper town claim. He continued that Buchanan is now encompassed, in part, by Knife River. Today's historical marker sits in what would have been the southwest corner of the platted town site. Maps contradict the bronze plaque, but the land office did sit very near the lake, immediately west of the St. Louis/Lake County lines. The exact spot may be under the highway.

During its heyday, Buchanan was home to many firsts, including the first newspaper, *The North Star Advocate.* It started as a semi-monthly publication and later became a weekly. It was last published in 1859 and no known copies exist. Other firsts included the first north shore post office. One first Buchanan most likely would not want to lay claim to was the first north shore ghost town.

As you travel the north shore, visit the site, dip your toes in the cool waters of the lake and visit the long ago site of Buchanan, the "Emporium of the North Shore."

Buchanan marker. (Author's collection)

CARSON LAKE

1910 - 1953

CLASS G

APPROXIMATE LOCATION:
Just west of Hibbing

It was just easier to have the workers live near the mines. Such was the thinking of early mining companies. Thus many towns, settlements and "locations" came into being and came to be located on company-owned land. Carson Lake, just west of Hibbing, was one such location. The hard-working immigrants, primarily from Serbia, Croatia, and Italy, built their homes and their lives at the sites. Even though the mining companies owned the land, they let the workers build their homes on the land. In the mid-1940s, when the companies wanted the iron ore reserves under the land, they began to remove the homes, and by 1952 only an open field remained. Carson Lake remained in the hearts and minds of its residents, including Carson Lake native, and Minnesota's only governor from the Iron Range, Rudy Perpich.

FRASER

1913 - 1972

CLASS G

APPROXIMATE LOCATION:
2 miles east of Chisholm

Once considered Minnesota's smallest city, back in 1913, Fraser was just another mining location, a true "company town." The land and the houses were all owned by the Oliver Mining Company, and all the residents worked for the company.

In 1931, Chisholm officials decided Fraser should be part of their city, which meant the mining company, as sole land owners, would pay a large share of the taxes. Company lawyers were called in, and the decision was made to incorporate Fraser as a city. One problem, a city had to have property owners, so Oliver Mining gave plats of land to ten residents, thus making it legal for Fraser to become a city.

In 1948, the Sherman mine, located very near Fraser was opened. As the mine expanded, land and homes were lost, fourteen homes at first. Folks assumed, correctly, that it was

only a matter of time before all of Fraser was lost to the encroaching mine. In 1972, the homes were offered to the tenants for the price of one dollar and by November of that year, all had been moved or torn down.

KITZVILLE

1913 - 1916 (1960s)

CLASS D

APPROXIMATE LOCATION:
2 miles east of Hibbing, now officially part of Hibbing

Originally its own entity, its own incorporated village, Kitzville has officially been part of Hibbing since it was annexed in the 1920s. The village was platted in 1907 and incorporated in 1912. Once incorporated, homes and businesses sprang up quickly. In 1911, the Kitzville School was built. The large, modern two-story building housed eighty students and included four classrooms, a principal's office, playroom, and two bathrooms.

Several mines surrounded the village and Kitzville itself was at the center of the contentious labor and union strikes of 1916.

Baseball was a popular community activity. It is said that when the Kitzville Creek overflowed, it was the largest skating rink in the entire region. In later years, Kitzville had no stores, no library, no post office, and no gas stations. It is now primarily a neighborhood.

Kitzville sign. (Courtesy of Elizabeth Urbach)

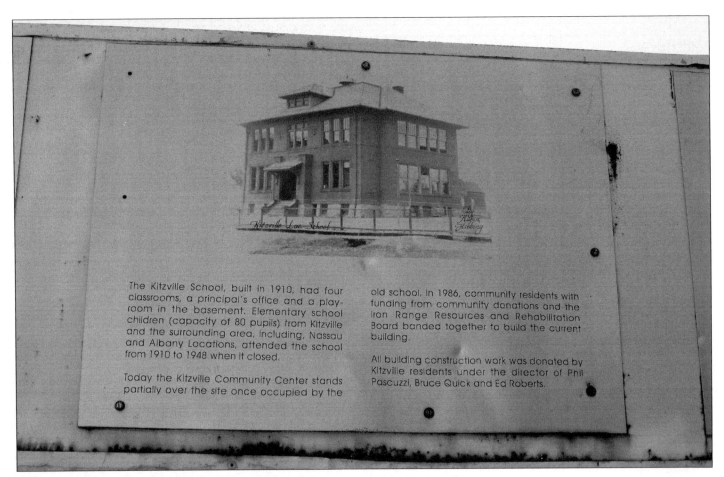

The Kitzville School, built in 1910, had four classrooms, a principal's office and a playroom in the basement. Elementary school children (capacity of 80 pupils) from Kitzville and the surrounding area, including, Nassau and Albany Locations, attended the school from 1910 to 1948 when it closed.

Today the Kitzville Community Center stands partially over the site once occupied by the old school. In 1986, community residents with funding from community donations and the Iron Range Resources and Rehabilitation Board banded together to build the current building.

All building construction work was donated by Kitzville residents under the director of Phil Pascuzzi, Bruce Quick and Ed Roberts.

Kitzville school historical marker. (Courtesy of Elizabeth Urbach)

Kitzville school site today. (Courtesy of Elizabeth Urbach)

In 1986, a new community center was constructed. It was built partially on the foundations of the school, which is fitting as Kitzville has always been community-minded. The community always built on the past preserving it for the future. Though no longer an incorporated village of its own, the Kitzville name and its warm neighborhood lives today.

Kitzville school foundations. (Courtesy of Elizabeth Urbach)

MITCHELL/REDORE

1917 - 1967

CLASS D

APPROXIMATE LOCATION:
2 miles east of Hibbing, north of U.S. #169 on Burton Road

Minneapolis and St. Paul aren't the only "twin cities" in Minnesota. Back in the early 1900s, St. Louis County had at least one set of adjacent communities including Mitchell and Redore. Divided in three sections, one was the yards (Mitchell Yards). Composed of a twelve stall roundhouse and repair shop, the yards was the primary staging area between Hibbing and the ore docks in Duluth. The other sections of the complex consisted of the company town of Mitchell, with a hotel and about twenty homes, and Redore, the residential area and settlement just to the west of Mitchell. Redore had homes designed especially for several men or small families. A hotel, two stores, and a school were also in Redore. Even though the physical location of the post office building was in Mitchell, the post office was established as Redore in 1917 and operated until 1967.

During World War II, Mitchell Yard was one of the busiest places around. The war effort required massive amounts of iron ore, and most of it came from the Iron Range by way of Mitchell. Reports say that the Mitchell Yards facility sent out three fully loaded trains at a rate of three per hour, twenty-four-hours a day. But alas, those days are gone.

When trains converted from steam power to diesel power in the early 1950s, the yards and Redore's days were numbered. By the mid 1980s, only two of Mitchell's forty plus buildings remained. Redore, as a town, was gone.

Mitchell Yards historic photo essay. (Courtesy of David Aho, www.mitchellenginehouse.org)

Mitchell Avenue. (Courtesy of Dan Turner, www.substreet.org)

Each year the Minnesota Preservation Alliance creates a list of the ten most endangered historic places in Minnesota. In 2011, Mitchell Yards made the list. In a stellar example of the present preserving the past for the future, preservation efforts are underway and ongoing. Longtime resident, David Aho purchased the Mitchell Yards site and is moving forward with plans to not only preserve the historical site but to also create a pre-vocational training center for students, with a focus on disadvantaged students. The mission is to provide hands-on training in an area that would provide life-long job skills. A diverse community group of advisors and mentors guide the program.

Dan Turner, of substreet.org, also chronicles the preservation effort. His stunning photography documents the site. You too can help preserve the site and foster the pre-vocational training center, check out www.mitchellenginehouse.org for more information.

Mitchell engine house. (Courtesy of Dan Turner, www.substreet.org)

Mitchell remains. (Courtesy of Dan Turner, www.substreet.org)

Redore. (Courtesy of Dan Turner, www.substreet.org)

Zim railroad depot. (Courtesy of – www.west2k.com)

SAX-ZIM

1916 – 1930 (Sax) & 1889 – 1990 (Zim)

CLASS A

APPROXIMATE LOCATION:
14 miles southwest of the City of Eveleth, near intersection
of St. Louis County Road #7 and #27

Sax was spelled many ways in its brief lifetime. The Duluth, Missabe and Iron Range Railroad called their station Sax and the Great Northern called their station Saxe. When the post office first opened it was called Wallace and later changed to Sax. The settlement was named for Solomon Saxe of Eveleth.

Zim was the site of a Duluth, Missabe and Iron Range Railroad station. It had originally been the site of a logging camp owned by a lumberman by the name of Zimmerman.

The area, encompassing both former town sites is now the home of the Sax-Zim Bog. The bog is a treasure trove for birding enthusiasts and is said to be home to over 240 species of birds including many rare northern birds such as the Boreal Owl and Northern Hawk Owl. Each year the bog hosts a three-day birding festival in February. Hiking trails provide access but much of the bog can be viewed from your vehicle.

Zim Post office 1990. (Courtesy of J. Gallagher, Post Mark Collectors Club)

Todd County

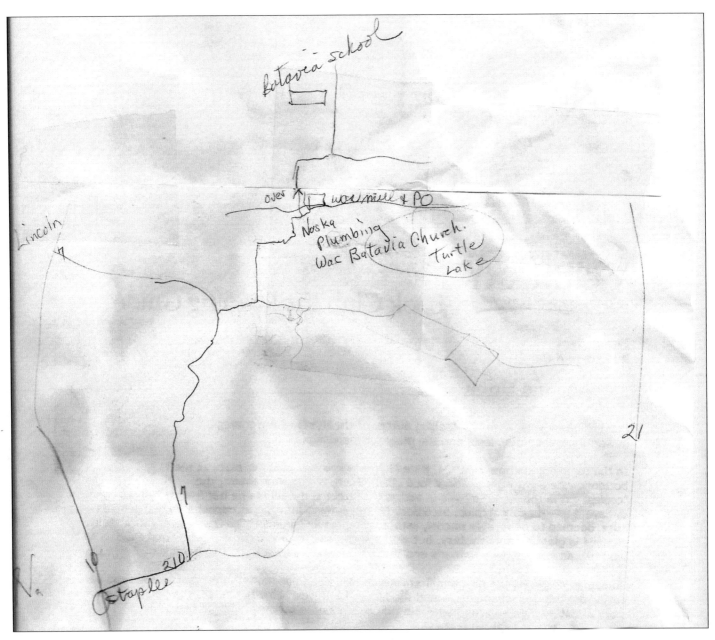

batavia school

over ↑ wax mill & PO

Noska
Plumbing
Was Batavia Church. Turtle
Lake

Lincoln

21

Va

10

Staples

210

Batavia map. (Courtesy of La Vonne Selleck)

Batavia school, two views. (Author's collection)

BATAVIA

1890 - 1904

CLASS A/G

APPROXIMATE LOCATION:
North of Peet Lake on Oak Ridge Road near Todd County #17

Looking at today's Turtle Creek, it's hard to imagine it capable of serving as a timber waterway. But back in 1878, it did. In fact, the creek supported the production of several thousand of board feet each day. Once home to two mills, the Todd County community of Batavia was located near the confluence of Turtle Creek and the Long Prairie River.

The first dam was at the mouth of Turtle Creek and was started by the Brower brothers, both Civil War veterans. Later the nearby community of Browerville was named for them. Still later a dam was constructed across the Turtle Creek one and one-half mile from the mouth of the creek. Known as Hart's Mill, Hart later moved to Browerville where he opened a store and lastly finally settled in Long Prairie.

A small community grew around the timber activity and within an approximately two mile radius of Peet Lake. A general store and a few other businesses made up the business district. Originally the settlement was known as Hart's Mill.

In the fall of 1879, one of Todd County's most gruesome murders took place in Batavia. Two recently arrived German immigrants were murdered in their cabin. The two guilty parties were apprehended. One was killed by an angry mob in Long Prairie and the other was sentenced to a life term in prison.

With all of the logging activity, the banks of Turtle Creek eroded and that eventually choked its flow. The mill had to be converted to steam power due to lack of a strong water source. Finally even the steam power wasn't enough, and the mill shut down. The mill pond grew over.

The community did have a church. In recent years, the church has been converted and now is home to Noska Plumbing. A post office also operated from 1890 until 1904.

In 1878 a school was built on donated land and was known as District #54. The white-frame building still stands. The cemetery, once overgrown has been restored and maintained by an area pastor and a Boy Scout troop from Staples.

Batavia, 2014. (Author's collection)

CLOTHO

1899 - 1908

CLASS D

APPROXIMATE LOCATION:
Intersection of Todd County Highways #3 and #38

The Civil War had just ended and times were hard, especially for those in the southern states who had fought with the northern army. Since Kentucky was a Confederate state, it was safer for the former Union soldiers there to move to the north. Given homesteads by the U.S. government, a group of Kentucky men moved to Minnesota, settling in the area that would become Clotho. When they arrived, they found a wilderness and Native American camps. Since timber was plentiful, the men built log homes. Money was scarce, so the abundant wildlife helped sustain their meager food supplies as did the native berries and nuts. Thus Clotho had its beginning.

Back in the late 1960s, approximately 1967, the sixth-grade class of the Clotho school, all four students, took on the task of researching and documenting Clotho history. They produced a small booklet that tells the story of Clotho and is one of the few area histories available today. Jeri Nelson, mother of one of the sixth-graders, Kali, very generously gave me a copy. Most of the information used in this summary is based on that school project.

Clotho, a name from mythology, was a busy community. A creamery was built in 1903 with the present standing building being constructed in 1920. The store was relocated throughout the community to several locations and had several owners. A 1966 fire badly damaged the store's interior, making it unusable. The creamery then offered a line of groceries. The town also had an auto repair garage and a dance hall. The dance hall hosted dances, creamery meetings, wedding showers, and more.

Religious services were offered by a variety of denominations and were conducted by several clerics. A Baptist church held services and Sunday School in the school building until the Baptist Church of Rose City moved to Clotho in 1938. In 1963 the church closed due to dwindling membership. The building stood on Jeri Nelson's property until just a few years ago, when it was torn down.

Several community groups were active in the community, including the Clotho Circle, which began in 1915. The ladies of the Circle organized community events, church suppers and ice cream socials. The town still hosts an annual ice cream

Clotho, 2014. (Author's collection)

Long ago Clotho business. (Author's collection)

Clotho creamery. (Author's collection)

Clotho today. (Author's collection)

United Methodist Church Clotho. (Author's collection)

social today. 4-H was also an active organization. In 1931 an annual Clotho picnic was started by the creamery. In later years a parade and the choosing of a queen were added. According to the booklet, one year over 5,000 people attended. In later years, the picnic ceased to exist.

Today some of the original buildings still stand and an active church (home of the ice cream social) are in the crossroads community. A few homes and residents are also in the settlement. Many longtime families still live in the area.

GUTCHES GROVE

1900 – 1940s

CLASS C

APPROXIMATE LOCATION:
Near intersection of Todd County Roads #10 and #11

Creamery, Gutches Grove. (Author's collection)

Up until a few years ago, the old creamery building was used by a printing company. The large majestic building still stands atop the hill on County #11 but it is no longer a business. Gutches Grove, today a quiet hamlet, was once a bustling community. Fern Haugen remembers her grandfather's store, the Marcyes Store. Her uncle owned a store in nearby Clotho. Gutches Grove also had a few other businesses including another store, a gas station a feed mill, and a two-room school.

Former creamery, Gutches Grove. (Author's collection)

Gutches Grove today. (Author's collection)

ROUND PRAIRIE

1879 - 1969

CLASS D

APPROXIMATE LOCATION:
Highway #27/71, four miles south of Long Prairie

Attracted by the abundance of virgin timber, the area's first settlers arrived in the 1850s and 1860s by covered wagon, oxcart, and by boat via St. Cloud. Others came for the farming opportunities.

One of Todd County's earliest towns, as the community grew, the need for a church became apparent. In 1882, after meeting in school buildings, the Round Prairie Community Church was organized. Obtaining a loan of $450.00, a church was constructed in 1899. All labor was donated by church members. One of the first pastors was Dr. Locke who had served in the Civil War. He not only organized the Round Prairie Church he was also instrumental in organizing several other Congregational churches in the region including Bertha and Staples. According to area historian Robert Thompson, securing chairs for the church was an obstacle. However, Dr. Locke found fifty chairs in Minneapolis. They were hauled on a horse-drawn hay rack the 125 miles to Round Prairie.

By 1919, Round Prairie included a blacksmith, grocery/dry goods store with a post office, a dance hall, restaurant, mer-

Early Round Prairie. (Courtesy of of S. Hewitt Collection)

165

cantile, machinery store and the church. The church is still standing. In 1941, a basement was added to the church and by then a creamery, sawmill, stockyard, and school had joined the community.

More than twenty rail cars a day left Round Prairie and carried a wide variety of goods, including pulpwood, lumber, eggs, butter, cattle, and hogs. A passenger train with two coaches and a mail car came through everyday heading for Sauk Centre north to Wadena. Passenger service stopped in the late 1950s to 1960s. The post office closed in 1969. The railroad land was sold in the 1980s.

Round Prairie is a peaceful roadside hamlet and the church is still at the center of the community.

Round Prairie Community Church. (Author's collection)

Round Prairie. (Author's collection)

Round Prairie building. (Author's collection)

Round Prairie today. (Author's collection)

BIBLIOGRAPHY

Aho, David. www.mitchellenginehouse.org. Web. December 24, 2014.

Aitkin County Historical Society, Heritage Book Committee. *Aitkin County Heritage*. Dallas. 1991.

Aitkin County Historical Society. *Aitkin County History and Recreation Guide*. Aitkin. 1996.

Alaska Township Book Committee. *Alaska Township: Then and Now*. Unknown. N.d.

Anderson, David E. *Moose Lake Area History*. Moose Lake. 1965.

Bailey, Carol. *Memories of Eastside Township, Opstead, Minnesota*. 1999.

Bates, Pauline. "The Village of Erdahl." *The Grant County Herald*. June 28, 1979.

Becker County Historical Society. "Ghost Towns of Becker County." Unpublished document. N.d.

Becker County Historical Society. *People's History of Becker County*. Dallas. 1976.

"Bena Victorius in fight for townsite." *The Bemidji Pioneer*. September 11, 1906.

"Marshall County History." Marshall County Historical Society files.

Bishop, Hugh. E. *By Water & Rail: A History of Lake County, Minnesota*. Duluth. 2000.

Blais, Judy. "Craigville." Email. August 19, 2014.

Blais, Judy. "Craigville: a glorious past." *International Falls Journal*. December 12, 1977.

Blais, Judy. "Craig: Population 500 and 26 roaring saloons." *International Falls Journal*. December 13, 1977.

Blais, Judy. "Wild and Wooly Life in Craig." *International Falls Journal*. December 14, 1977.

Cass County Historical Society. *Cass County Heritage*. 1999. Dallas/Walker.

"Center Valley, Minnesota – 1920s and Yesterday!" http://heschhistory.blogspot.com May 31, 2009. Web. October 15, 2013

Cook County Historical Society. "Colvill." Email. December 21, 2014.

Cordes, Jim. *Pine County . . . and its memories*. North Branch. 1989.

"Creamery Fire." *Staples Headlight*. July 15, 1910.

Crow Wing County Historical Society. "The Story of Gorst's Mill." March 11, 1995.

Debs Daily Doers Homemakers Club. "Roosevelt Township, Past and Present." Unknown. N.d.

Deer River Area Centennial History, 100 Years Great in Ninety-Eight. Deer River. 1998.

Diebel, Lynne Smith. *Paddling Northern Minnesota: 86 Great Trips by Canoe and Kayak*. 2005.

Drache, Hiram M. *Koochiching, Along the Rainy River Frontier*. Danville. 1983.

Exley, Perry. Old Clitherall. Email September 9, 10, 2014.

Faust, Maurice. *Aitkinsville to Zerf*. 2002

Fisher, Harold L. *The Land Called Morrison*. St. Cloud. 1972.

Geving, Renee. "Cuba." Email. November 14, 2014.

Goligowski, Verna. "History of District #54." Unknown. N.d.

Gould, Hallie M. "Old Clitherall's Story Book: A History of the First Settlement in Otter Tail County, Minnesota 1865–1917." Unknown. N.d.

"The Gorst Mill Site." Minnesota Archeological Site File. Spring 1978.

"H. Lutien Burial Services Today in Backus." *The Walker Pilot*. November 6, 1936.

Hanson, Willma. "McHugh." Personal Interview. September 10, 2014.

Hanson, Willma. "McHugh." Phone. September 12, 2104.

Hasin, Steve. "Immigrant descendants restore Russian church." *Hometown Focus*. September 3, 2010.

Hawkinson, Susan. Jewett, Warren. *Timber Connections*. Grand Rapids. 2003.

Helga Township. "Nary Community History." Unknown. N.d.

Hinnenthal, Ruth. "Pontoria Store." Letter. December 13, 1997.

"History of Royalton." www.hillbillyblue.com Web. February 22, 2013

Holden, Thomas. "Oshawa." Phone interview. July 24, 2014.

Houser, Donna. "Nary Community Band celebrates 50th year." *Bemidji Pioneer*. August 12, 1981.

Iverson, Eileen. "Gorstville." Letter. May 8, 1989.

Kangas, Judy. "Lawler." Phone interview. July 25, 2014.

Kimball, Jim. "Peggy Mattice and Craigville." *Minneapolis Star and Tribune*. January 30, 1972.

Koochiching County Historical Society. "History of Koochiching County." Dallas. 1983.

Kremer, T. Email. September 12, 2014.

Kremer, T. "Horton, Latona." Email. October 25, 2014.

Kujala, Cindy. "Remains of the Past." *Hometown Focus*. April 4, 2014.

LaBlanc, Stella. *The First Cross*. St. Cloud. 1970.

Lake of the Woods County Historical Society. *Lake of the Woods County, A History of People, Places and Events*. East Peoria. 1995.

Lake Park Association (Historical Society). *History of Becker County*. Dallas. 1976.

Lakewood Lodge. www.lakewoodlodge.com

Lamppa, Marvin. *Minnesota's Iron Country: Rich Ore, Rich Lives*. Duluth. 2004.

"Leader, Center of Farming Section." *The Walker Pilot*. February 26, 1925.

"Leader Synopsis." Unknown. N.d. Files of Cass County Historical Society.

LeVassuer, Andrea. Email. July 3, 2014.

"The Little Bramble Church Celebrates." *Grand Rapids Herald*. www.grandrapidsmn.com. August 23, 2011.

Luukkonen, Larry. Phone interview. July 25, 2014.

Luukkonen, Larry. "Judy's Journal: Origins of a hometown chronicle." *The Aitkin Age*. December 14, 2013. Web.

Lynch, Jack. "Man with a Mission. Years of Yore." *Hibbing Daily Tribune*. June 5, 2011.

Marchand, Louis. *Up North, Beltrami County's Townships*. Bemidji. 1998.

Mattice, Peggy, Esse, John. "Forest History Oral History Project." Interview. July 8, 1975. http://collections.mnhs.org/cms/display.php?irn=11124743

Mayo, Katherine and William. *61 Gems along Highway 61*. Cambridge. 2009.

"Memories of Butler." East Ottertail History Museum. Unknown. N.d.

Mitchell, Frank. "Latona-Horton." *Hubbard County Historical Society Newsletter*. Park Rapids. March 2007.

"Monowheels." www.monowheels.com Web. September 24, 2014.

Nelson, Gary. McHugh. Email. September 14 &15 2014.

Norgard, Irene Hill. *Larsmont Yesterday*. 1969. Reprinted 2012.

Nute, Grace Lee. *Rainy River Country*. St. Paul. 1950.

"Old Clitherall." www.Justicetwo.com Web. December 14, 2014.

"Old Town Resort." www.oldtownresort.com Web. December 13, 2104.

Olson, Patty. "Erdahl." Ca. 1990. Grant County Historical Society.

O'Reilly, Bill & Dugard, Martin. *Killing Lincoln: The Shocking Assassination That Changed America Forever* New York. 2011.

"Oshawa Store Keeper Perishes in Snow Storm." *Cass County Pioneer*. November 4, 1936.

Park Rapids. http://parkrapids.com

Petrowske, Alfred J. "On the Trail." Bemidji. 1989.

Rachey, Hilda. "North Country." *Up North*. Bemidji Historical Society Newsletter. Vol. 5, n.3. (1992)

Red Top Facebook Page. https://www.facebook.com/redtopmn

Robbins, Don. Interview. October 1, 2014.

Robbins, Don. *Wahkon: A Town Remembered*. 2012.

Roesler, J.T. "Aggie K. Jelstrad Closes Erdahl Restaurant." *The Grant County Herald*. Ca. 1986.

Roseau County Historical Society. *County of Roseau Centennial 1895-1995*. Roseau. N.d.

Rottsolk, James E. *Pines, Mines, and Lakes The Story of Itasca County, Minnesota*. Itasca County. 1960

Rutz, Lenny and Betty. "What life was like at the Gregory Depot." Files of Morrison County Historical Society. N.d.

Saint Mary's Church. www.stmarys-twoinlets.com

Sandvick, Glenn N. "Land Office Buchanan: Emporium of the North Shore." *Minnesota History*. Fall 1991.

Schmidtbauer, John."Center Valley." Email. July 13, 2014.

Sebasky, Marlys Hesch. "Center Valley." Email. October 10, 2013

Selleck, LaVonne. "Batavia." Interview. September 25, 2014.

Selleck, LaVonne: "Batavia" Letter. October 1, 2014.

Sixth Grade Class, Clotho School. "District 2293, Clotho, MN." Unknown. 1967.

"Store at Oshawa Burns to Ground; Little Is Saved." *Cass County Independent*. June 26, 1931.

Stulich, Patty. "Two Inlets." Phone Interview. December 15, 2014.

Sundberg, Lillian. "History of Discontinued Post Offices." *Grygla Eagle*.1984.

"Tales of the Old Home Town!" *The Cass Lake Times* March 6, 1952.

Trunt, Leo. *Beyond the Circle*. Baltimore. 1998.

Trunt, Leo. *Prosper Can you tell me*. Baltimore. 1993.

Turner, Dan. "Ghost Towns of the Arrowhead." *Zenith City*. December 1, 2014.

Turner, Dan. "Ghost Towns of the Arrowhead." *Zenith City*. December 15, 2014.

Upham, Warren. "Minnesota Place Names" http://mnplaces.mnhs.org.

Urbach, Elizabeth. "Kitzville." Email. January 4, 2015.

Von Alman, Charlotte. "Silverdale, Rauch, Bramble." Marceline. N.d.

"Vote will decide fate of Nary School Building." *The Bemidji Pioneer*. www.helgatownship.com Web. June 29, 2014.

Wall, Randy. "From lost to found . . ." *The Aitkin Age*. October 5, 2013.

Welle, Duane. "Belle Prairie." Phone Interview. December 15, 2014.

Welle, Duane. "Belle Prairie." Email December 23, 2014.

Weston, Fern Holden. "Old Houses of the Oshawa Area." Unknown. N.d.

White, Jesse. "Kitzville: Now sort of a neighborhood of the city to the west." *Mesabi Daily News*. March 18, 2008.

Wollum, Gerald. Email. July 4, 2014

Wollum, Gerald. Email. July 15, 2014.

Wollum, Gerald. Email. December 5, 2014.

Wollum, Gerald. *Track and Timber: The History of Red Top, Minnesota*. 1991.

Zaffke, Betty. Personal letter. July 25, 2014.

Zaffke, Betty. "Oshawa Store and Post Office." Unpublished Memoir. Cass County Historical Society. June 11, 1991.

Zaffke, Betty. "Oshawa." Phone Interview. July 24, 2014.

INDEX